Anonymous

Explanation of the Sacrifice

and of the liturgy of the Mass

Anonymous

Explanation of the Sacrifice
and of the liturgy of the Mass

ISBN/EAN: 9783337335519

Printed in Europe, USA, Canada, Australia, Japan

Cover: Foto ©Lupo / pixelio.de

More available books at **www.hansebooks.com**

EXPLANATION

OF THE

SACRIFICE AND OF THE LITURGY

OF THE

MASS.

BY A PRIEST.

"The Mass being the chief act of divine worship,
"the Council of Trent enjoins all pastors to instruct
"their flocks in the nature of it, and in all that relates
"to it, that they may be assiduous in assisting thereat,
"and devout in reaping the fruits thereof."—*Sess.* xxii.
ch. 8.

SECOND EDITION, ENLARGED AND IMPROVED.
SOLD FOR THE BENEFIT OF ORPHANS.

LONDON:
THOMAS RICHARDSON AND SON;
DUBLIN AND DERBY.
LONDON: BURNS AND OATES—E. J. FARRELL.—DUBLIN: DUFFY.
NEW YORK: HENRY H. RICHARDSON AND CO.
MDCCCLXX.

Nil obstat quo minus imprimatur.
W. G. TODD, D.D.

Imprimatur :

✠ HENRICUS EDUARDUS,
Westmonasteriensis.

APPROBATION OF THE SECOND EDITION.

The Oratory, May 4th, 1870.

My dear Mr. ———

I thank you for your very interesting book on the Mass, which came to me a day or two ago.

It is *full of instruction as well as interest*. I cannot doubt it will have a good sale, and will satisfy the pious intentions, and the anxiety and care, of which it is the fruit.

It is a great pleasure to me to find myself thus in your remembrance. Give me your good prayers, and believe me

Sincerely yours in Xt.,

JOHN H. NEWMAN.

APPROBATION OF THE FIRST EDITION.

Rev. dear Sir,

Your discourses on the Mass state the doctrine of the Catholic Church on that head in most clear and intelligible terms, and enforce it with great zeal and earnestness. I trust that they will induce the faithful to be assiduous in assisting at the Holy Sacrifice, and to rejoice in the many graces which, by their piety and devotion, they can secure through the efficacy of the Adorable Sacrifice, in which, each day, the merits of the Sacrifice of the Cross are applied to our souls.

Yours sincerely in Christ,
✠ THOMAS GRANT.

St. George's, Jan. 16th, 1864.

TESTIMONIALS.

Rev. dear Sir,

I have read your useful little book, and think it simply and clearly written. I have no doubt but that it will be of great service, especially to persons entering the Church.

ERRATA.

Page 75, line 24, read "Moses, who by the command of God had committed the law to writing, ordered a sacrifice to be offered up; and having read the words of the covenant in the hearing of the people took the blood of the victim," &c.

Page 114, line 2, for "by Him and with Him," read "by Christ and with Christ."

Page 189, lines 17 and 19, erase the word 'Again'

" 199, line 1, for 'passin' read 'passing'

" 223, line 3, for 'intreat' read 'entrea'

" 276, line 15, read 'the order of nature was not observed, since man did not contribute to it.'

APPROBATION OF THE FIRST EDITION.

Rev. dear Sir,

Your discourses on the Mass state the doctrine of the Catholic Church on that head in most clear and intelligible terms, and enforce it with great zeal and earnestness. I trust that they will induce the faithful to be assiduous in assisting at the Holy Sacrifice, and to rejoice in the many graces which, by their piety and devotion, they can secure through the efficacy of the Adorable Sacrifice, in which, each day, the merits of the Sacrifice of the Cross are applied to our souls.

Yours sincerely in Christ,

✠ THOMAS GRANT.

St. George's, Jan. 16th, 1864.

TESTIMONIALS.

Rev. dear Sir,

I have read your useful little book, and think it simply and clearly written. I have no doubt but that it will be of great service, especially to persons entering the Church.

Believe me,

Yours faithfully in Christ,

H. E. MANNING.

Bayswater, August 29th, 1864.

My dear Rev. Sir,

I feel much the kindness you have done me in sending me your volume. I set a great value on it as coming from so well-read a theologian.

I am, my dear Sir,

Very truly yours in Christ,

JOHN HENRY NEWMAN,
Of the Oratory.

The Oratory, Birmingham,
Sept. 19th, 1864.

Rev. dear Sir,

I beg to thank you for your kindness in sending me a copy of your little work on the Holy Sacrifice. I have read it through, and have been extremely struck with its similarity, almost its identity, with a short course of instructions on the same subject, which I delivered to our students in the autumn of 1861, and again taught more in detail to our upper classes, last year, and which a friend of mine has been delivering to another congregation this Lent. I think we must have been reading the same books before we wrote our respective instructions, among others, Nicholas' *Etudes Philosophiques*. My four discourses contain all that I have read in yours, omitting the first. I have, on the stocks, another series of lectures, dealing at greater length on the subject of your sixth. Under these circumstances, I need not say how glad I am to see them in print.

I remain, Rev. dear Sir, with much respect,
Yours very truly in Christ,
J. SPENCER NORTHCOTE,
Principal of Oscott College.

Oscott College, Birmingham,
March 1st, 1864.

Rev. dear Sir,

Your book on the Mass has, by a second and more careful reading, in every respect immensely gained in my estimation. I cannot help writing to you to pour out my earnest and sincere admiration of its erudition, logic, and piety.

Yours, &c.,
DENIS FLORENCE MCCARTHY,
Co-editor of the *Month*.

Winsley Manor House,
Bradford-on-Avon, Somersetshire,
April 13th, 1864.

OPINION OF THE CATHOLIC PRESS.

"This little book, to our knowledge, *is the only one in the English language that treats of the nature of the Sacrifice of the Mass*. Other treatises explain the different parts of the Liturgy of the Mass; but not the nature of the Sacrifice thereof. It is highly spoken of and recommended by bishops and theologians of the day. Written, as it is, in a plain, earnest, and impressive style, it cannot fail to be of great benefit to all who read it in a proper spirit. The sublime nature of the Sacrifice is forcibly dwelt upon in this eloquent work, which we sincerely recommend to our readers."—*Tablet*, April 13th, 1864.

CONTENTS.

	PAGE
Preface: On the importance of being well instructed in the Mass	1
Preamble	7

PART I.

ON THE SACRIFICE OF THE MASS.

CHAPTER I.

On Public Worship; its obligation, necessity, and advantages ... 9

CHAPTER II.

Sacrifice in general; its nature, origin, necessity, and perpetuity ... 27

CHAPTER III.

On the nature of the Sacrifice of the Mass.—The Sacrifice of the Altar one and the same with the Sacrifice of the Cross; a continuation, a representation, and a commemoration thereof ... 49

1.—The Sacrifice of the Mass is the continuation of the Sacrifice of the Cross ... 56

		PAGE
2.—The Mass is a real representation of the Passion and Death of Christ	...	64
3.—The Mass is a commemoration of the Sacrifice of the Cross; yet so as to be really that which is commemorated	...	65
Prayer	...	72

CHAPTER IV.

The Sacrifice of the Mass a true and proper Sacrifice ... 73

CHAPTER V.

On the fruits of the Mass ... 101
    Des Intentions dans lesquelles on doit dire ou entendre la Sainte Messe ... 118

CHAPTER VI.

The excellence of the Sacrifice of the Mass ... 125
Prayer ... 144

CHAPTER VII.

On the Ceremonies, Language, Vestments, Incense, Lights, &c. used in the Liturgy of the Mass ... 145
On the Ceremonies of the Mass ... 146
On the Language of the Liturgy ... 147
On the use of particular Vestments or Robes during the Mass ... 152
On the use of Incense ... 153
On the use of Holy Water ... 155
On Altars ... 157
On the Tapers which are lit up during the Mass ... 158

PART II.

EXPLANATION OF THE LITURGY OF THE MASS.

CHAPTER I.

	PAGE
On the importance of worthily assisting at the Mass	161
On the intentions and dispositions with which we ought to assist at Mass in order to reap the fruits thereof	163

CHAPTER II.

Explanation of the component parts of the Liturgy of the Mass ... 166

ARTICLE I.

Preparation of the People.

The Penitential subdivision	167
The Confiteor	170
The Instructive subdivision	178
The Introit	178
Kyrie Eleison	181
Gloria in excelsis Deo	184
Dominus Vobiscum	188
The Collect	192
The Epistle	195
The Gospel	198
The Creed	201

Article II.

	Page
Preparation of the Matter of the Sacrifice.	207
Offertory	208
Mixture of the Wine and Water	212
Continuation of the Offertory—Simultaneous Oblation of the Bread and Wine—Suscipe sancta Trinitas	216
Orate Fratres	218
The Secret	221
The Preface	222

Article III.

The Canon.	229
First Prayer of the Canon—Te Igitur	231
Second Prayer of the Canon—Memento of the Living	233
Infra actionem	236
Third Prayer of the Canon—Communicantes	237
Fourth Prayer of the Canon—Hanc Igitur	240
Fifth Prayer of the Canon, which immediately precedes the Consecration—Quam Oblationem	244
The Consecration	247
First Prayer after the Elevation	254
Second Prayer after the Elevation	257
Third Prayer after the Elevation—Supplices Te Rogamus	258
Fourth Prayer after the Elevation—Memento for the Dead	260
Fifth Prayer after the Elevation, and the last of the Canon—Nobis quoque peccatoribus	263
Conclusion of the Canon	266
On the Devotion with which we should assist at the Holy Sacrifice	269
The Real Presence of Jesus Christ in the Eucharistic Sacrifice, proved from the Testimony of the Holy Fathers of the Primitive Ages of Christianity	272

ARTICLE IV.

	PAGE
The Communion, or fourth and last part of the Liturgy	279
Preparation for the Sacrificial Communion	281
The Lord's Prayer	282
The Pax Domini and the prayer Hæc commixtio, together with the accompanying ceremony	284
The Agnus Dei	288
Three Prayers in immediate preparation for the Communion of the priest:	
First Prayer	292
Second Prayer	294
Third Prayer	295
Domine non sum Dignus	296
Communion of the Priest	298
Communion of the faithful no essential part of the Sacrifice	299
Communion of the faithful a Divine Precept	300
Daily Communion in the Primitive Church	301
Spiritual Communion	303
Dispositions for a Spiritual Communion	305
Thanksgiving after Communion	306
Anthem called the Communion	308
Post Communion	309
Ite, Missa est—Depart, the Divine Service is now over	310
Placeat Obsequium	311
Last Blessing	312
Last Gospel	314
Summary or Resumé	318

EXPLANATION OF THE ENGRAVINGS.

The first Engraving represents the Death of Jesus Christ, which is to all mankind the source of all mercy, grace, and salvation.

The Second Engraving represents Jesus Christ instituting the Sacrifice of the Mass, in order to communicate to all the members of His Church the fruits of the Sacrifice of the Cross.

The third Engraving represents the Priest, as minister of Christ, imparting to the members of the Church, by means of the Mass, the fruits of the Sacrifice of the Cross.

ERRATUM.

At foot of Engraving facing page 161, for '*C. Nice, Sess.* 22,' read '*Con. Trid. Sess.* 22, c. 2.'

PREFACE.

ON THE IMPORTANCE OF BEING WELL INSTRUCTED IN THE MASS.

"God," says Christ, "is a spirit, and they who adore Him, must adore Him in spirit and truth." (S. John iv. 24.) *In spirit*, that is, with a knowledge of the nature of the worship we render Him: *in truth*, that is, with all the sincerity of our hearts. But the Mass is the principal act of Divine worship; we must therefore understand it, and join with all our hearts and souls in offering it up.

St. Peter warns all Christians to be ever ready to give an account of their faith, and of the motives of it. "Be ever ready," says he, "to satisfy every one that asketh you the reason of the hope that is in you." (1 Epist. iii. 15.) This warning particularly regards the Sacrifice of the Mass, which is a principal Christian mystery, nay, an abridgment of all mysteries.

"Let your worship," says St. Paul, (Rom. xii.) "*be a reasonable one*." In order to this, we must understand the nature of sacrifice in general, and of the Sacrifice of the Mass in particular; we must know what are the intentions and dispositions necessary in order that the Mass may become vailable to us.

"*This is,*" says Christ, "*eternal life, that they may know Thee, the only true God, and Jesus Christ whom Thou hast sent.*" (S. John xvii. 3.) But Christ is not only our Redeemer and Mediator, but also our Sovereign High Priest and Victim. For the sacrifice of Himself which He offered up on Mount Calvary, did no more expire by His death than did His Priesthood. The whole victim was restored to Him at His resurrection, and He carried it up into the sanctuary of heaven, at His ascension, and with it He continually pleads before the throne of His Father, for the obtaining of mercy, grace, and salvation for us.

Before His departure from this world, *He ordained others, not as His successors, (for His Priesthood is eternal,) but as His ministers, to keep up this same sacrifice in His Name and in His Person in His Church; He Himself invisibly officiating as High Priest and Victim, both as offerer and offering, and keeping up a continual succession of them all days, even till the consummation of the world.*

All our good is derived from the sacrifice of the cross: it is the fountain of life, and the source of all grace. "There is (says à Kempis) no "health of the soul, no hope of eternal life, but in "the cross of Jesus Christ. There is no justifica-"tion nor salvation for us except through the "merits of Christ's Passion and Death." (bk. ii. 12.) But the Mass is the principal channel for conveying to our souls the merits of the Sacrifice of the Cross. The death of Christ on the Cross only made us capable of redemption, while the Sacrifice of the Mass puts us in possession thereof. In order therefore, to obtain a share in the merits of Christ's Passion and Death, it is necessary to be well instructed in the Mass.

It is only by means of the Mass that we are enabled *adequately* and *worthily* to render to God the four great duties that we owe Him, of adoration, thanksgiving, atonement, and impetration. But, in order to this, we must understand the dignity and efficacy of the holy Sacrifice. *Ignoti nulla cupido.*

Tepidity, routine, and negligence are the bane of religion. "Cursed," says the Prophet Jeremias, (xlviii. 10.) "is he that does the work of God negligently." But the Mass is God's most excellent work, the worship which He has appointed to be rendered to Himself alone, the only worship which is acceptable to Him: but in order to perform it acceptably, a competent knowledge thereof is indispensable.

Hence, he that has not this competent knowledge, cannot be said to know his religion.

Hence, in order to derive benefit from assisting at the Mass, it is necessary to know what is then taking place on the altar, and how to join in it in spirit; it is not enough to read from beginning to end the prayers called *Devotions for Mass,* as if they were a mere formulary of prayers.

Hence, there is in this matter, a degree of ignorance which is guilt, and which prevents those who labour under it, from hearing Mass as they ought. They must at least know what is the meaning of the consecration and elevation; when they take place; and what they themselves should then do. They must know when the communion is, what the Priest is then doing, and what they themselves should then do.

Unless they know this, they are in culpable ignorance of their religion, and incapable of rendering to God the supreme homage they owe Him.

Many persons there are who, though but imperfectly instructed in the Mass, are nevertheless punctual and devout in assisting thereat, and derive considerable benefit from it, and who, if fully instructed in all that relates to it, would assist at it, with a greater degree of respect, awe, and devotion, and thence derive much greater benefit.

Why are many Catholics so negligent and so irreverent in assisting at the Holy Sacrifice, but because they were not instructed in it in their youth, or did not avail themselves of the opportunities they had of obtaining a competent knowledge of it? To such, might it not be said:—the worship you perform without understanding, that I will endeavour to explain to you. (Acts xvii. 23.)

Were Christians nowadays as well instructed as the primitive Christians were; had they as lively a faith in the sacred mysteries as they had, would they not be most anxious to avail themselves of this price of their Redemption? Would they not be urgent for the voice of that blood that speaketh better things than the blood of Abel, to plead for them with the Eternal Father? (Heb. xii. 24.)

It would be deplorable that even one single well disposed person should all his life be frequenting the holy sacrifice without knowing its excellence and the fruits to be derived from it; or that any one should, through ignorance, have neither respect nor confidence in it: yet are there not many such?

Where such ignorance prevails, it is difficult to expect that religion can make much progress. Is not therefore the Mass the anchor of our hope? Is it not then of primary importance that it should be fully understood and appreciated by all? However necessary a knowledge of the Mass is, it is not alone sufficient to make us duly appreciate it; for its excellence is only perceptible to the eyes of an enlightened faith: "the things "that are of God," says St. Paul, "no one knows "but the Spirit of God." (1 Cor. ii.) "To the "man, destitute of a lively faith, the things of God "appear as foolishness; he cannot understand "them. But our Heavenly Father will un- "doubtedly bestow His Holy Spirit on them that "ask Him."—"I am," says He, "He that teach- "eth knowledge, and giveth a more clear under- "standing to little ones (to the humble and clean "of heart) than can be taught by men. I am He, "that, in an instant, elevates an humble mind to "comprehend more reasons of eternal truth than "can be acquired by many years' study." (A Kempis, book 3, ch. 43.)

We must therefore, fervently and perseveringly, implore of God to enlighten our minds to comprehend the dignity and efficacy of this august Sacrifice, to set it before our mind's eye in its proper light, and to make us believe in it with an undoubted faith, which will inspire us with awe, and render us diligent in reaping the fruits thereof. For unless our minds are enlightened from above, we shall not behold the *Invisible* present on our altars, as if He were visible; nor shall we be penetrated with that profound sense of the Divine Presence, which made the Patriarch Jacob exclaim: "The Lord is in this place, and I knew "it not! How awful is this place! It is no other "than the House of God, and the gate of Heaven." (Genesis xxviii.)

PREAMBLE.

We are not to confound the Sacrifice of the Mass with the Liturgy of the Mass. The Sacrifice of the Mass was instituted by Jesus Christ personally, (St. Matt. xxvi. 20, &c.): whereas the Liturgy of the Mass was drawn up by the inspired apostles immediately after Pentecost, in accordance with the instructions they had received from their Divine Master, especially during the forty days He remained upon earth after His resurrection. The Sacrifice consists of three parts : the Consecration, the essential Oblation, and the Communion; while the Liturgy has four parts—the preparation of the people, the preparation of the matter of the Sacrifice, the Canon, and the Communion.

Hence, this treatise consists of two parts : 1st. On the Sacrifice of the Mass : 2nd. On the Liturgy of the Mass.

EXPLANATION OF THE SACRIFICE,

AND OF THE

LITURGY, OF THE MASS.

FIRST PART.

ON THE SACRIFICE OF THE MASS.

CHAPTER I.

ON PUBLIC WORSHIP; ITS OBLIGATION, NECESSITY, AND ADVANTAGES.

"When two or three are gathered together in My name," says Christ, "there am I in the midst of them." S. Matt. xviii. 20.

"How lovely are Thy tabernacles, O Lord of Hosts! My soul longeth and fainteth for the courts of the Lord. Thy altars, O Lord of Hosts, my King and my God. Better is one day in Thy courts, above thousands." Ps. lxxxiii.

"Let us provoke one another unto charity, not forsaking our assemblies, but comforting one another." Heb. x. 24.

"Strive," writes St. Ignatius, martyr, to the Ephesians, "to hold assemblies together to pay to God the homage of thanksgiving and praise due to Him. For when you often meet in the same place, the power of Satan is broken; he is weakened, and the destruction he endeavours to bring upon us, is kept off by the concord of your faith."

It is an indispensable obligation incumbent upon man, as a rational creature, endowed with free will, and created by God, and for God, frequently to acknowledge His supreme dominion over him, and to testify his essential dependence on Him. It is the first law and the first debt of our nature. For being created *by Him*, it is our duty to serve Him: being created *for Him*, it is our duty to seek Him: and being redeemed *by Him* for regaining the happiness we had forfeited, it is our duty to love Him. Hence Christ says: "The Lord thy God shalt thou adore, and Him only shalt thou serve. Thou shalt fear the Lord, and serve Him only." (St. Matt. iv. 10.)

God complains of those who neglect this greatest and first of all duties. "The son," says He, "honours his father, the servant fears his master: "if I am a Father where is My honour? if I am a "Master where is the fear of Me?" (Malachi i. 6.) "I have," says He, "brought up children; but "they have despised Me. The ox knoweth his "owner, and the ass his master's crib; but Israel "hath not known Me, and My people have not "understood." (Isaias i.)

Nay, God's original design in creating man was that He might honour and praise Himself; for when He had finished the creation of this world, and put together its several parts, there was still wanting therein an intelligent creature, that could apprehend the beauty and order of His works, read in them the traces of His infinite wisdom, power, and goodness, honour Him and pay Him a tribute of praise. Irrational and even inanimate creatures, by bearing the impress of the Deity, pay Him a mute homage of praise. "The heavens show forth the glory of God, and the firmament declareth the work of His hands." (Ps. xviii.) But a rational and spiritual homage was due to God. Man was therefore created, endued with powers capable of understanding and acknowledging the unlimited perfections of the Author of all things, and placed in the temple of this world, as the priest of nature, to offer up to God the incense of praise and thanks, both for himself, and for the whole creation, particularly for that part which, being mute and insensible, was incapable of this duty in a spiritual manner. By our understanding we know and acknowledge God; and our will, the fountain of gratitude, prompts us to make to Him, to the best of our power, a rational return by love, praise, and thanksgiving.

But it is not enough to praise and thank God privately; we are bound frequently to offer Him a *public* homage. God is as much the Creator and supreme ruler of empires, kingdoms, cities, and lesser societies, as He is of individuals. His dominion over them and their dependence on

Him, is as essential, complete, and inalienable as His dominion over individuals and as the dependence of individuals upon Him.

Empires, kingdoms, cities, &c., as public bodies, owe therefore to God public worship, as much as individuals owe to Him private worship. The like motives engage us to return to God public homages of thanksgiving and praise: His blessings we enjoy in common; the same sun gives to all light and warmth; the fatness of the earth is for all; we are all partakers of God's graces, of His wonderful redemption, and of the comforts of His holy providence. For all these benefits, which He has heaped upon us in common, we must join to offer Him a public sacrifice of thanks. Hence David says: "In the midst of the church I will praise Thee, O God: with Thee shall be my praise, in the great congregation." (Psalm xxi.)

God, in creating us, destined us to live in society. A certain instinct and our mutual necessities link us together. Society is our element, out of which we can no more live, than fish can live out of water.

But without laws, there can be no society; without morality there can be no laws; without religion there can be no morality; and without public worship there can be no religion. Public worship is necessary to maintain in the world a sense of God, and of our obligations to Him; without which all society would soon dissolve and come to an end. The extreme insensibility of the generality of mankind as to their obligations and spiritual interests, arises from their being totally absorbed in the cares, anxieties, and pleasures of this life. The remedy of this evil is assiduous meditation on the life to come, and spiritual exercises, as religious festivals, public worship, and public instruction. To make mention of public instruction alone, it is the great means of conveying to mankind, and inculcating on their minds and hearts the knowledge of their duty to God, to their neighbour, and to themselves, together with that of the sanction of those divine obligations by future eternal rewards and punishments; and thus inspire them with a sense of God and of religion and promote the peace and harmony of society.

Accordingly, no set of men ever formed themselves into a religion, true or false, without public worship; so strongly is this duty engraved on the hearts of all men, by the author of our nature. Puffendorf, the greatest of all writers on natural and public law, inculcates the duty of public worship; and Addison observes, that even if the keeping of the seventh day were but a human institution, still, it would be the best method that could be devised for civilizing mankind. Even deists acknowledge the duty of public prayer. "Reason, (says Hobbs,) directeth, not only to wor- "ship God in secret, but also and especially, in "public, and in the sight of men; for without this, "the procuring of others to honour God is not "effected. It is the voice of nature, says Tindal, "that God should be publicly worshiped." Hence the wisest legislators and founders of states have ever made public worship an essential part of their civil constitutions.

Public worship is more honourable to the Divine Majesty, more advantageous to our neighbour, and more profitable to ourselves than private worship.

1st. Public worship is more honourable to God than private worship; all the faithful closely united together, with their pastor at their head, and infinitely above them Christ Jesus the great Mediator of the New Testament, form but one body; when they present themselves before God, their homage is most honourable and most acceptable to Him, as a king receives much greater honour from the homage done to him by a whole city or by all the states of his kingdom in a body, than by that which private individuals could offer him singly.

In private worship, we honour God by the high esteem we conceive and testify of His excellency. But we more properly do Him honour when in public worship, we declare before others and in the sight of heaven and earth, our unutterable esteem, acknowledgment and deep sense of His sovereign perfections. It is particularly then, that we give Him the honour due to His name. Hence the Angel Raphael said to the two Tobiases: "Give glory to the God of heaven, in the sight of all that live."

Public worship is more edifying than private worship to our neighbour, kindling in him a desire to love and serve the great God of all creatures, and to invite angels and men to adore Him, to whom they owe all that they are and have. It supports a belief of His existence, a deep sense of His Majesty, and devotion in the world. By it we more powerfully invite and engage others to serve God than we could do by words; by publicly glorifying God, we exercise the functions of apostles, thereby propagating His worship among many, for His greater glory upon earth and for the salvation of souls during all eternity. It is particularly on the tender minds of children, that the sight of a multitude of people, including their parents, prostrate before God, with hands and eyes raised up towards heaven, makes the most salutary impressions. They are formed to public worship by the example of those whom they love and revere; and they will continue to worship God publicly, when their parents are no more. Even the most backward and dull are stirred up to fervour and devotion, at the sight of so many devout persons adoring God together. Who is there that at such a sight would not feel moved to prostrate himself in like manner to worship the Lord of all things, and to make to Him the same acknowledgments? The fervent themselves feel their devotion increased, and are filled with spiritual joy, on beholding so many persons blessing the common Lord and Father of all with their whole hearts, and in perfect union. Such joy would enlarge the hearts of all who have any feeling of divine zeal and charity. Hence the Psalmist calls, not only upon men, but on all creatures, to praise with him the Lord with their whole hearts. "Behold, (says David,) how good and pleasant it is, for brethren to praise God in union." (Ps. cxxxii.) God showers down all sorts of blessings upon people who are united in His praises. Longum iter per preceptum, breve per exemplum.

Public prayer *is more beneficial to ourselves than private prayer*. If our public homage is more honourable and acceptable to God, and more beneficial to our neighbour, in like manner, petitions put up by the whole church are more powerful than private prayer in obtaining divine blessings. It was a maxim of the ancient synagogue, that the prayers of the congregation are always heard; but not so assuredly those of individuals. Our

Lord, by bidding us to say in prayer, *Our Father,* puts us in mind that we are frequently to join in public prayer. "God," says St. Thomas Aquinas, "often grants to one man's prayers that which he "asks; but to many who unanimously join in the "same petitions, He grants more willingly, more "largely, and more freely." The requests of great cities or nations are a kind of suppliant compulsions that are not ordinarily rejected; and the efficacy of the prayers of the whole Church is all-powerful with God.

All prayers offered by the ministers of the Church, as its public representatives, derive a particular virtue from their public character and functions, and from the faith and devotion of the universal Church, in whose name they are offered. The priests are mediators between God and His people, and their advocates with Him, being appointed to make Him a tender of their homage, to offer Him thanks, to avert His anger, and to draw down upon them His mercy and blessing. The efficacy of their ministry is exceedingly increased by the actual presence and union of their congregations with them. By this union, the weakness and the defects of the dispositions of some, are supplied by the fervour of others; and whilst all pray in the same spirit, they form but one voice and one prayer which Christ our Mediator and Head presents and so strongly recommends, by the price of His adorable blood, that it offers to God a holy and agreeable violence.

This singular efficacy, absolute necessity, and indispensable obligation of public prayer, were the voice of reason and nature silent, appear evident, from God's having made it a particular object of His religious laws in every dispensation of revealed religion; from His having appointed for it regular times, places, and ministers; and instituted sacrifices, to be there and then offered up to Himself. By a particular providence, He has always provided, for the honour of His divine name, a Church of faithful believers and worshipers, that He might be glorified throughout all ages; and He has directed, by express revelations and commands, that all should honour Him by public worship. Thus, after that God had punished our first parents for their pride and disobedience, through compassion on them, He exempted them from labour on the seventh day, and taught them to keep it holy, by offering up sacrifices.

During the antediluvian period, it was by public worship and by public instruction, that religion was kept alive and perpetuated; for Enos the son of Seth exerted himself in propagating the public worship of God by assembling large masses of people, offering up sacrifices in their presence, and in their behalf, by explaining to them the nature and obligation thereof, and teaching them thereby to obtain from God their spiritual wants and necessities. After him, Enoc the sixth descendant from Adam, likewise went about, assembling multitudes of people, instructing them and impressing on their minds the great truths of religion, and their obligations to God, to their neighbour, and to themselves. But, as after those two holy patriarchs there arose no successor to their zeal, sacrifices and public instruction were soon neglected; ignorance, error and disbelief crept in, and were soon followed by every kind of vice and wickedness, which brought on the punishment of the universal deluge, in which the whole human race, with the exception of one family, perished. This shows the necessity of public worship, and of public instruction.

The Israelites, while in Egypt, were prevented from having public worship, being condemned to hard labour on the Sabbaths as on other days. But after their departure out of Egypt, and during the forty years of their wandering in the desert, God, in order to impress on their minds the obligation of abstaining from work on the seventh day, and that they might consecrate it to His worship, showered down on them a double portion of manna on the sixth day, while none fell on the seventh day. This heavenly food would keep from sunrise on the sixth day, till sunset on the following day; whereas, on other days, it would keep only from sunrise to sunset of the same day. When they became so numerous as to form a nation, God gave them laws, and public instructors, and established public worship among them. He instituted four kinds of sacrifices, corresponding with the four principal duties they owed to Him; by His appointment the ordinary daily sacrifices offered up in the temple were doubled on the seventh day.

Why did God from the commencement of the world, forbid all servile works on the seventh day? Why did all legislators and founders of states make it an essential part of their civil constitutions, but that all might be enabled to meet in public worship to honour God and draw down on themselves His help and protection? Why did God prefix the word *remember* to the third commandment, and not to any of the others, but to intimate that if this commandment be duly observed, it will greatly help us to observe all the others; and that if it be neglected, the other commandments will, in like manner, be neglected and forgotten.

But as under the Mosaic Law, sacrifice could be offered up in the temple of Jerusalem only, and as the people dispersed throughout Palestine, were required to assist at the sacrifice in Jerusalem only at the three great yearly solemnities, those alone who dwelt at Jerusalem, enjoyed the advantages of weekly public worship. To all the other Israelites, the sabbaths were merely days of rest and of private devotion. It was by private instruction that the knowledge of the truths of religion and of the commands of God were perpetuated; the parents instructing the children as Moses had commanded them: "these words," said he, "which I have commanded thee this day, "shall be in thy heart; thou shalt tell them to "thy children, thou shalt meditate upon them "sitting in thy house, walking on thy journey, "lying down and rising up." Yet for want of weekly public worship and weekly public instruction, the nation, during the eras of the judges and of the kings, was continually relapsing into idolatry. But after the Babylonish captivity, Esdras, the second legislator of the Jews, in order to prevent the recurrence of a similar catastrophe, had, by divine inspiration, places of public worship, corresponding with our parish churches, called *synagogues*, erected in every canton throughout the length and breadth of the land, where people might meet on every sabbath, to pray, to read the Scriptures, and to listen to the interpretation of them by the priests and Levites; but not to offer up sacrifices. The result was most beneficial; the people who had hitherto lived in ignorance and violation of the covenant, became the most uncompromising enemies of every idolatrous practice, and until the destruction of the temple and the dispersion of the nation, continued faithful observers of the law of Moses, notwithstanding that Antiochus and others, by violent persecutions, endeavoured to make them abandon it: witness the glorious death of the aged Eleazar and of the mother, with her seven sons; witness the noble stand in defence of the law of God, made by Judas Machabeus and his brothers.

In the new law, Jesus Christ, the Apostles, the Councils, and the holy Fathers likewise impressed on Christians the duty of public prayer, and recommended it, as a most powerful and necessary means of perpetuating religion and obtaining all manner of graces.

1st. Christ inculcates upon us this duty *by word and by example*. After His return from Egypt, and during His private and public life, He never missed being present at Jerusalem on the solemn occasions prescribed by the law. Although the fear of Archelaus prevented Him from residing at Jerusalem, the fear of God brought Him thither on the days commanded by the law. He inculcated public prayer by word. "When," says He, "two or three are gathered together in My name, "there am I in the midst of them," in My quality of High Priest, animating them by My example, presenting their prayers to My Eternal Father, pleading for them, by showing the marks of My wounds, by which I have purchased for them a title to all mercy and grace. The primitive

Christians always sanctified the Sundays by meeting together to celebrate and receive the Holy Eucharist, and to listen to the explanation of the Word of God. Thus we read in the Acts of the Apostles (ii. 42), " That they *were persevering in* " *the doctrine of the apostles,* and in *the communi-* " *cation of the breaking of bread.*"

In offering up the Holy Eucharist, St. Paul prescribes "that in the Church, first of all, suppli-
" cations, prayers, intercessions and thanksgivings,
" be made for kings and for all that are in high
" stations, that we may lead a quiet and peaceable
" life in all piety and chastity; for this is good
" and acceptable in the sight of God our Saviour."
(1 Tim. ii.) S. Justin Martyr, in the second century, says in his Apology: " Upon Sundays, all
" that live in the city or in the country meet
" together in the same place and at the same
" time, when the writings of the prophets and
" apostles are read, as much as time will permit.
" The bishop then makes a sermon, in which he
" instructs the people, and animates them to the
" practice of the good precepts; all, afterwards
" rise up and pray. Prayers being over, the Holy
" Eucharist is celebrated, and the bishop puts up
" prayers and thanksgivings with all the fervour
" of which he is capable, and the people conclude
" by the acclamation '*Amen.*' The consecrated
" elements are then distributed and partaken of by

"all present, and sent to the absent, by the hands "of the deacons." Pliny the Younger, writing to the Emperor Trajan, states, that the Christians were wont to assemble before sunrise to sing hymns to their Christ, and to encourage one another to abstain from all manner of evil deeds. St. Peter, whose very shadow cured the most inveterate diseases, stood indebted for his deliverance from prison to the joint prayers of the faithful: for "prayer "was then made for him without ceasing by the "Church." (Acts xii. 5.) St. Paul had constant recourse to the supplications of the faithful, to obtain the Divine blessing on his labours. "If "we are weak," says St. Chrysostom, "when we "pray alone, we become powerful when assembled "together in a body. By our union we overcome "God. You can indeed," says he, "pray at "home, but such prayers will not have the same "power and efficacy as when the Church, in a "body presents supplications with one heart and "one voice; and the priests, being present, offer "up the words of the whole assembly. Peter and "Paul are the pillars and towers of the Church; "yet it was the joint prayers of the Church, that "broke asunder the chains of the former, and "opened the mouth of the latter." Tertullian, speaking of Christians assembled in public prayer, says: "We come in a formidable body and close "battalion, as it were, to do violence to God and

"to storm heaven by the voice of united prayer:
"such a force offers a most agreeable violence to
"heaven." "Nothing," says St. Athanasius,
"better represents the concord of a people;
"nothing more powerfully inclines God to hear
"our prayers than great assemblies of persons,
"making supplications together, and singing the
"divine praises with one heart and one voice; for
"if two persons united together in prayer obtain of
"God what they ask, what may we not expect
"when a numerous people join together in the
"same place and answer *Amen* to all the prayers
"of the priest?"

So great was the spirit of zeal of the primitive Christians for public Divine worship, that they could not be deterred from assisting at the celebration of the Divine Mysteries. Hence, in the reign of the Emperor Valerian, many Christians were kept in loathsome dungeons, loaded with chains, purposely to prevent them from assisting at public worship; and many others were put to death for having assisted thereat. SS. Saturninus and Dativus, having been apprehended while assisting at Divine worship on a Sunday, answered the judge, under the sharpest torments:
"The obligation of Sunday is indispensable. We
"never pass a Sunday without meeting together
"to pray: it is not lawful for us to omit the
"duty of that sacred day."

Wherefore, to neglect the sanctification of the Sunday by public prayer, is to trample on a most solemn precept of God, inviolable throughout all ages; it is to refuse to employ the most necessary means of sanctifying our souls, and rendering to God the solemn worship we owe Him. The primitive Christians stood in need of no other stimulus to engage them to fulfil this sacred duty, than their ardour and devotion, and a sense of piety and religion. But when the fervour of many began to wax cold, the Church, by an inviolable law, commanded all her children to assist attentively and devoutly at Divine worship, on all Sundays and days of obligation. The Council of Trent, in particular, (Sess. xxii.) enjoins all bishops to take care that their flocks be duly put in mind of the obligation every one is under, of assisting at public worship on the above days, and of hearing the word of God expounded and inculcated.

CHAPTER II.

SACRIFICE IN GENERAL; ITS NATURE, ORIGIN, NECESSITY AND PERPETUITY.

"All things, according to the law, are cleansed with blood (with sacrifices); and without the shedding of blood (without sacrifice), there is no remission of sins." (Heb. ix. 22.)

Public worship is a duty which we owe to God; and sacrifice, the proper means of performing that duty. It is the great act of public worship: by its nature, it is the public worship of God.

From the first, God required that men should render Him some common acknowledgment of His supreme dominion over them, and of their essential dependance upon Him;—and sacrifice, not common prayer merely, but solemn sacrifice was the act of divine worship which He appointed for this purpose. It was He Himself, that revealed to our first parents this mode, by which He desired to be approached and worshiped by them, and by their descendants. Hence, wherever man exists, we find sacrifice everywhere prevalent. Hence, since the creation of the world, sacrifice has ever formed the chief feature of that religion which God gave to man. It has been ever considered to be emphatically the worship which God required to be rendered to Himself alone. No religion, either natural or revealed, ever existed without it. Sacrifice and religion, sacrifice and divine worship, have always been looked upon as one and the same thing. They who would worship God acceptably, must offer up sacrifice to Him.

In its most general acceptation, sacrifice is an honour due to God alone, and the principal honour due to Him. *It is an honour due to God alone;* it belongs to Him exclusively; it is uncommunicable to any other, being expressive of the supreme dominion, belonging to Him alone. To offer it to any other, would be the crime of idolatry. Hence, God Himself says: "He that sacrificeth to the gods, save only to the Lord, shall be put to death." (Exodus xxii. 20.) Sacrifice is the *highest worship* that we can render unto God. There are two species of worship due to God alone, adoration and sacrifice, of which, the latter is the greater. Adoration is the personal worship of God, even when domestic, or public, as in Catholic afternoon divine service. Sacrifice is the public worship of Him. We can alone adore God at any time, and in any place. Sacrifice, being the public worship of God, requires a church or temple, a priest, an altar, an offering, particular robes, and the presence of a congregation of people, in whose name and in whose behalf, the sacrifice is offered. In adoration, we humble our persons, our souls and bodies only before God; in sacrifice, we moreover make Him an offering of something material and tangible. By adoration, we offer Him our actions only: by sacrifice, we offer Him not only our actions, but also our very beings.

The offering made to God in sacrifice is always *destroyed* or consumed, 1st. in acknowledgment that we are God's creatures, and as nothing in His sight; that we owe to Him, life, breath and all things: "Behold," says David to God, "it is Thou that determinest the number of my "days; and my substance is as nothing before "Thee." (Psalm xxxviii. 6.) 2nd. To acknowledge that God is so perfect and independent, that He does not stand in need of our offerings, and cannot be bettered by them: "I have said to the Lord, Thou art my God; Thou hast no need of my goods." 3rd. That He is the Master of life and death: "The Lord killeth and maketh alive, "He bringeth down to hell and bringeth back "again. The poles of the earth are the Lord's; "and upon them He has set the world." (Anna's Canticle.)

The destruction of the offering or victim, is the distinctive and indispensable feature of sacrifice, and is consequently found in every kind of sacrifice. By sacrifice, we acknowledge that we are God's creatures. But did we ever reflect what it

...for is offered
...ledge that
...e ever reflec

is to be God's creatures? to owe to Him our being; at one moment to be nothing, and the next to exist by the sole will of God; so that, were He to will it, we should in an instant, become nothing again, as we were before He made us? Nothing stands to us in the place in which we stand to God; nothing we possess, whether it have life or not, is ours, in the sense in which we are God's. The animal we kill, the fuel we consume, the food we eat, have their existence independently of us; but we, as they also, have no existence out of God. It is not only that God is great and strong, and that we are little and weak; but that we exist only by the act of God's Will. It is not only that we are God's property, and that He has the power of life and death over us; but that out of Him, we are nothing. Words cannot express the reality of this tremendous truth; God is all, and we are nothing. Thus, not only all we have, but all we are, is His: this debt we owe to God, by the very fact of our existence. Hence, we see, what the worship of God by sacrifice is. It is to offer ourselves to Him, to make an entire surrender of ourselves to Him, to annihilate ourselves before Him.

If mankind had never sinned, if we had been born into this world as innocent and as holy as Adam was before his fall, nothing less than sacrifice could have satisfied the debt we owe to God, as to the author of our being, the All-holy, Almighty, Eternal God. By the destruction of the offering, men showed that they owed all to God, and were as nothing in His sight. But the shedding of blood is something more. An unbloody sacrifice, for instance, a sacrifice of corn and wine, is such a sacrifice as an innocent creature might make to his Creator. But we are no longer in that blessed state: when Adam fell, we lost our innocence; when Adam sinned, we became sinners; we all sinned in him, and as sinners, became subject to death, the punishment of sin. A bloody sacrifice is therefore the offering of sinful creatures to their offended God. Our state was changed: before we owed to God the homage of our being; now we owe to Him the additional penalty of death. Not only so, we had incurred a debt which nothing we had to give, could satisfy. God was angry with us; we were guilty in His sight; we stood in need of forgiveness and reconciliation. How were they to be obtained? In His love and mercy, God provided a remedy. At the very moment when He pronounced upon our first parents the sentence of punishment, He told them of a Deliverer to come, for whose sake, He would pardon them and their children. This Deliverer was none other than our Saviour Jesus Christ, the Second Person of the adorable Trinity, who was to become man and die for us.

But God did not merely foretell them of this deliverer; He taught them a religious rite, by which they might have a present interest in the work He was to do, and, as it were, forestall the benefits of His death. This religious rite was sacrifice. It prefigured the great propitiatory sacrifice of the cross. It was no longer merely the solemn act of worship, by which our first parents offered themselves to God and paid Him the homage they owed Him as His creatures; by bloody sacrifices, they moreover acknowledged themselves to be sinners, made expiation for sin, and obtained forgiveness.

In what, then, does sacrifice, as offered by sinners consist? It consists of three parts: of the offering to God of a victim; of the immolation of it; and of its destruction or consumption.

1. *Of the offering of a victim:* An animal is brought to the temple; the priest places, in his own name and in that of those for whom the sacrifice is to be offered, his hands on its head; thereby acknowledging that they had, by their sins, incurred the penalty of death, declaring that they transferred their sins on to its head, and substituted it to die in their place: they at the same time fervently prayed that God would remit the forfeit of their lives in consideration of the faith, contrition, and devotion with which they offered up the sacrifice.

2. *In the immolation of the victim:* Bloody sacrifices date from the fall. How significant were such sacrifices of the sinner's condition before God, and of his needs! The victim he slew, whose blood he poured out, whose body he burnt and consumed, represented himself. By those several acts he acknowledged the debt which, as a sinner, he owed to God; that his life was forfeited for his sins, and that suffering would be his eternal portion, should God deal with him according to his deserts; at the same time, he testified his faith in the promises of God, together with his steadfast hope, that the true Victim, the Lamb without spot, would one day come and restore him to the favour of his Maker. God said to him: "Thou art guilty; thou deservest "death; thou must acknowledge it; thou must "slay victims, and thereby acknowledge, that it is "thou thyself that deservest to be slain. In the "place of thyself, I will accept of the blood of "animals; I will exempt thee from the death "thou hast incurred; and I will pardon thee the "crimes by which thou hast rendered thyself "liable to eternal punishment."

3. The third essential part of sacrifice is *Communion,* or the participation of the victim. That the flesh of the victim should be partaken of by those who assisted at the sacrifice, was commanded by God Himself, in revealing to man this rite. It

is a universal conviction, derived from the primitive revelation made to man, and which has ever existed among all mankind, that by partaking of the flesh of the victim, they actually communed with the Divinity. This participation of the flesh of the victim, has always been practised by all the nations of the earth. "Throughout the "whole world," says Pelisson, "the flesh of the "victim has always been eaten: amongst all "nations, the sacrifice has always ended by a "solemn banquet of man with the gods." Hence we find, in the ancient poets, mention of the banquets of Jupiter and of the meats of Neptune; meaning that the flesh of the victims was eaten, after it had been offered to those false divinities. Among the Jews, the sacrifice of holocaust, in which alone the whole victim was burnt in acknowledgment of God's supreme dominion over them, and of their total and essential dependence on Him, was accompanied by the offering of a cake, to be eaten as a communion, that this indispensable condition of sacrifice might not be wanting.

Sacrifice is not, therefore, like Protestant worship, merely a form of prayers, something being *done* there as well as *said*. Protestant ministers perform no priestly office whatever; they turn always to the people, and face them in praying, as in preaching. They do nothing, indeed, which any one man might not do just as well as another.

Sacrifice is necessary: it is the indispensable act of religion. It is as impossible to conceive a religion without sacrifice, as to conceive God without sovereign dominion over His creatures, and His creatures without the obligation of acknowledging His sovereign dominion over them. He is the Creator and Ruler of all things, the principle, the source or fountain of all the natural and supernatural advantages we enjoy. To Him, therefore, we owe the homage of whatever we are and have; and the only means of performing this homage is sacrifice; for His sovereign dominion over His creatures cannot be fully recognised but by their destruction. They, therefore, who would worship God acceptably must offer up to Him sacrifices.

Sacrifice is of Divine origin or institution: Almighty God continued His mercy to our first parents after their banishment from paradise. He not only exempted them from labour on the seventh day, but also taught them to spend it in offering up to Him in sacrifice some part of the produce of their fields, or of the increase of their flocks, in token that all they got by their labour, was His gift; and in token of His supreme dominion over all His creatures. God had also a further intention, that the shedding of the blood of the lamb or other animal that was killed and burnt upon the altar, should serve as a token that in due time the Blood of Jesus Christ, the Son of God, should be shed on the cross for the sins of all the guilty children of Adam. "For it was impossible that with the "blood of oxen and of goats, sins should be "remitted." (Heb. x. 4.) It was God Himself that showed to Adam the manner of sacrifice; how they were to build an altar, and how the gift that they offered thereon, was to be burnt, for fire is the punishment of sin. Had not God Himself revealed to them the manner of this rite, and declared that it was thus He wished to be honoured and appeased, how could they have imagined that an animal slain in their own place could deliver them from punishment and death, and that God accepted this substitution? Those bloody sacrifices were pleasing to God only as figures of One who was to come to be offered Himself in sacrifice, and whose own blood was to be the redemption of the world. In this way, then, Almighty God showed His love and mercy to our first parents, in teaching them how to preserve their fear and regard for Him, and how to offer to Him such sacrifices and worship on His holy day of rest as He was pleased to accept, in the meantime, until Jesus Christ should come into the world to leave behind in it the true and only acceptable Victim which is now offered in the holy Sacrifice of the Mass.

It is plain, from what has been said, First, that no sacrifice, whether bloody or unbloody, had any power in itself to take away sins, or to draw down blessings from God; it had this power only, as being a type or figure of the sacrifice of Christ. The real victim of propitiation was Jesus Christ, thus slain in figure and promise. It was the death of the Lamb of God, slain in figure from the beginning of the world, that the patriarchs and ancient just celebrated beforehand in their bloody sacrifices. It was to express their faith and hope in the future Sacrifice of the Cross that they offered up bloody sacrifices; it was their faith in this future Sacrifice, that rendered their sacrifices acceptable to God, and imparted efficacy to them. Without this faith, no sacrifice could have been acceptable to Him.

2. It is also plain that no sacrifice can be acceptable to God unless accompanied, on the part of the worshiper, with the interior sacrifice of the heart, by faith, contrition, and devotion. It is vital religion, the religion of the heart, that renders both the worshiper and the sacrifice acceptable to God; for while man sees but the things that appear outwardly, God looks to the dispositions of the heart: "for God is a "spirit, and they who adore Him must adore

"Him in spirit and in truth." (St. John iv.) Exterior sacrifice is but the outward expression of the interior sacrifice of the heart; it would be the greatest hypocrisy, outwardly to profess dispositions, which one does not inwardly possess. If God condemns those who offer Him sacrifice negligently, how much more will He condemn those who merely pretend to honour Him: hence He complains of those who pretend to "honour "Him with their lips, while their hearts are far "from Him." This does not mean that the interior sacrifice of the heart, without the exterior sacrifice of the altar, is sufficient. The sacrifice of the altar was God's institution and ordinance. It was the means by which mankind were to have an interest in the future Sacrifice of the Cross. It was the way in which He desired to be approached and worshiped by His people. It is therefore necessary to assist worthily at exterior sacrifices, in order to become acceptable to God; and those only are thereby benefited who offer them, and assist at them, with the requisite dispositions of faith, contrition, and devotion. They were, moreover, obliged to assist at exterior sacrifices, in order to provoke their neighbours to worship God by their example. In a word, exterior sacrifice has always been regarded by mankind, as the means of testifying towards the divine Majesty the dispositions of their hearts.

The religion which God gave to man, at the creation, was a religion of sacrifice; sacrifice was the religion of the antediluvian period, of Abel, Seth, Enos and Enoc; the religion of Noah and of his sons, the religion of Melchisedech and of Job was a religion of sacrifices.

When God took the family of Abraham to be His own peculiar people, among whom His true worship was to be preserved, and of whom should be born the promised Saviour, He instituted a regular order of priests, to whom alone it appertained to offer up sacrifices: thus, He set aside the tribe of Levi for the service of the altar, and the family of Aaron for the office of the priesthood. He instituted four different kinds of sacrifices, corresponding with the four great duties we owe to God. 1. Holocausts, or whole burnt offerings. 2. Thank offerings. 3. Sin offerings. 4. Peace offerings. Those four different kinds of sacrifices comprise all the ends of divine worship: 1. to render supreme honour and glory to God; 2. to give Him thanks for His innumerable benefits; 3. to appease His anger, and to obtain from Him the pardon of our sins; 4. to ask of Him those graces and blessings of which we stand in need. In the holocaust, the victim was entirely consumed by fire, while in the other three sacrifices it was only partly consumed; of the rest the priest and people partook, thus making it a kind of spiritual banquet or communion. In the first seven chapters of the Book of Leviticus, we read how God commanded His chosen people to worship Him; how, in some way or other, sacrifice was the one great action of their lives. It was one continual round, or offering up of sacrifices, daily, every day, and on every occasion, public and private: the fire of the altar was never suffered to go out; the smoke of the sacrifices ascended continually; the blood of the victims never ceased to flow round about the altar. Every morning and every evening, incense was burned and a lamb offered up as a holocaust to God. On the Sabbath the offerings were doubled: every new moon was made holy to the Lord by still more abundant sacrifices; and all the great festivals were solemnised in a similar manner throughout the year. More than this, sacrifice was not only the national religion; it was the religion of the individual man. It was associated with every circumstance of his life. If he committed any sin, he confessed it and offered up sacrifice for it; he led the victim to the priest, and laid his hand upon its head, to show that the innocent animal was going to bear his sins, and to die in his place; it was then slain by the priest, and its blood poured round about the altar. If he desired to obtain any particular blessing or mercy he did in like manner; if the blessing were granted, or any particular mercy bestowed upon him, sacrifice was offered up in thanksgiving. Now this Jewish religion was the religion which God gave to His people; and which was to prepare them for Christianity. The Jewish religion was Christianity in the bud or germ. Its object was to educate and to train men for the Christian religion. The Jewish religion was Christianity undeveloped, while Christianity is the Jewish religion developed and fulfilled. But if Christianity was to have no sacrifice, how could the Jewish religion be a preparation for it? So far from Judaism being a preparation or introduction to Protestantism, it is essentially and absolutely opposed to it.

Sacrifice was no *distinctive mark* of the Mosaic religion. It was universally practised among the nations of the earth. It is certain, as well from holy Scripture as from profane history, that not in one country only, but over the whole inhabited earth, there were priests and sacrifices. "If," says Plutarch, "you travel through the nations of "the earth, you may meet with cities without "walls, without lyceums and academies, without "a monetary circulating medium, without arts "and sciences; but you will never meet with a "city without gods, temples, priests, sacrifices, "oracles, and religious ceremonies; in a word, "sacrifice has ever been the religion of the whole world."

It is true that, while the nations of the earth retained the use of sacrifices, they lost the true meaning of them; that they lost sight of the object of them; that they forgot, or but dimly remembered, *Him* who was to come, and sacrificed to false gods, and to idols, instead of to the one true and living God; but, still, while misapplying them, they retained correct notions of the nature of the rite, and continually offered it up.

Sacrifice was never to cease: it commenced with the world, and is to cease but with the world. We have seen above, that it is of divine institution, and that from the beginning, it has nvariably been, among all nations, the principal and essential act of divine worship. This, alone, is a strong presumption that God designed that it should always be continued to be offered up. We nowhere find it written in any part of Scripture that all kinds of sacrifices were to cease. On the contrary, we find it asserted that they should continue as long as the world should last.

Carnal sacrifices, the sacrifices of bulls and goats, were indeed to be done away; but another, and a better, sacrifice was to come in their place. The Christian Church was to have a real sacrifice, offered on real altars, by real priests. God had predicted, by His prophets, the abolition of the Jewish sacrifices; and Christ did abolish them: but He announced, at the same time, the coming in of another sacrifice. Thus Isaias (xix. 19) declares that there shall be "an altar of the "Lord in the midst of the land of Egypt, and "that the Egyptians shall worship Him with "sacrifices and offerings." It is here expressly foretold that the Egyptians, a gentile people, should have the altar of the true and living God among them, and should worship Him with sacrifices and offerings. The same prophet also foretold (lxvi.) how God would cast off the nation of the Jews, and call in the gentiles in their place. "I will," says He, "send to the gentiles, of "them that will be saved; and I will take of "them to be priests and Levites, saith the Lord: "for as the new heaven and the new earth, which "I will make to stand before Me, so shall your "seed stand and your name." Here again it is declared that, not only the Christian Church shall have priests, but that *they shall endure as long as the heavens and the earth shall stand.* "There "shall not," says Jeremias, (xxxiii. 17,) "be "cut off from David a man to sit upon the throne "of the house of Israel, neither shall there be "cut off from the priests and Levites a man "before My face, to offer holocausts, to burn "sacrifices, and to kill victims continually." These words evidently apply to our Blessed Lord and His Church; for the Angel Gabriel, (St. Luke i. 32,) when he announced to the Blessed Virgin that she should become the Mother of the Messias, applied them to Him; and they evidently declare that the priesthood shall never fail, but that, in that Church or kingdom, there shall ever be priests to offer up sacrifices continually.

We read in the eleventh verse of the first chapter of Malachy, the following famous prophecy, in which God says to the Jews: "I have "no pleasure in you, saith the Lord of Hosts: " and I will not receive a gift from your hands. "For, from the rising of the sun to the going "down thereof, My name is great among the "gentiles; and in every place there shall be "sacrifice, and there shall be offered to My "name a clean oblation: for My name is great "among the gentiles, saith the Lord of Hosts." Two things are here clearly foretold: 1st. the rejection of the Jewish sacrifices; "*I have no plea-* "*sure in you*, and I will *not receive a gift from* "*your hand:*" 2nd. the substitution of a new and better sacrifice in their place, which was to be offered up, not only in Jerusalem, but in every place: "*and in every place there shall be sacri-* "*fice, and a clean oblation.*" This future sacrifice cannot be that of the cross, which was offered once only, and in one place, namely, in Jerusalem, but that of the Mass, which is continually offered up everywhere.

If we consider the words of our Lord to the Samaritan woman, (St. John iv.) in connection with the above prophecy of Malachy, we shall discover that they mutually illustrate each other. The woman, acknowledging Christ as a prophet, desires to have her mind set at rest on the long disputed question, which divided the Jews and her own people: "Our fathers," said she, "wor-"shiped on this mountain (Garizim); but You "say that Jerusalem is the place where men must "adore." By *worshiping*, or adoring, is here meant the offering up of sacrifice; for the word *adoring* is frequently used thus in Scripture; sacrifice being emphatically the worship of God. Indeed, all men have ever been at liberty to adore God, in the general sense of the word, wherever they pleased; but sacrifice could be offered only in the place which God had chosen. Our Saviour answered her: "Woman, the hour cometh, when, "neither on this mountain, nor in Jerusalem, "you shall adore the Father." That is to say, the hour is close at hand, when the sacrifices of both Jews and gentiles shall be abolished, and the adoration of the Father by sacrifice shall not be confined to this place or to that, to this mount or to Jerusalem; but shall be extended to every place. Christ moreover adds: "The hour is "come when true adorers shall adore the Father "in spirit and in truth." This part of the prediction tells of something new; but true adorers had always adored God in spirit and in truth, as the words are commonly understood. For good Jews and Samaritans had always worshiped and served God sincerely; there would have been nothing new in this: something more must, therefore, be intended, namely, that the time is at hand, when sacrifice will be offered up to the true and living God, in every place throughout the world, from the rising of the sun, to the going down thereof. Sacrifice will, therefore, never cease till the end of the world.

Protestants maintain that these prophecies refer to the Sacrifice of the Cross; that the old sacrifices were abolished, and that Christians have no other sacrifice but that which Christ offered of Himself upon the Cross.

Most true: the old sacrifices were abolished, and the Sacrifice of Christ upon the Cross is the Christian's only sacrifice. But how can the Christian be said to have that sacrifice, which was offered eighteen hundred years ago; to have it now, in present possession, to-day, and every day? The Sacrifice of the Cross was offered up on one particular day, in one place, on Mount Calvary, outside the walls of Jerusalem. But the sacrifice of which the prophets speak, was to be offered "among the gentiles, and in every place;" not once only, but continually. If it be answered, that the Christian has it by faith, I reply: so had the Jews, so had the patriarchs. Yet faith could not give it to them as a present possession; neither can faith alone give it to the Christian. Thus the Protestant, on his own showing, is in no better condition than was the Jew. Nay, he is plainly in a worse; for the Jew had the figure of a true sacrifice, which was all he could have, before the offering was made; he had that which, by God's appointment, gave him an interest in the sacrifice that was a preparing; but the Protestant has nothing but the barren memory of the event. How, then, can he be said to have an interest in an oblation of which he has no share in offering? In what sense the Catholic possesses the reality, I will show in the sequel. *Sacrifice, therefore, will never cease to the end of the world.*

What, then, shall we think of Protestantism, which has no sacrifice, which took upon itself to abolish the great Christian sacrifice; which did away with that which everywhere, and in all times, and by all Christians, throughout the world, has always been regarded as the highest and most essential act of divine worship? Every other religion, since the commencement of the world, has had sacrifice. Protestantism is the only religion without sacrifice; and as Protestantism is only three hundred years old, it is only for the last three hundred years of the world, that this strange sight has been beheld of a people believing themselves to possess a divine religion, and yet a religion without a sacrifice.

Thus, it was God Himself that revealed sacrifice to our first parents as the mode by which He was pleased to be worshiped by them, and by their posterity. Sacrifice has in all ages ever formed the principal feature of the religion of all the nations of the earth; and it will continue such till the expiration of all time.

"This is my body.... This is my blood of the new testament, which will be shed for many for the remission of sins." — *St. Matthew* xxvi.

"In the Mass the principal Priest and the Victim are the same as on the Cross."—*Con. Trid. Sess.* 22, c. 2.

CHAPTER III.

ON THE NATURE OF THE SACRIFICE OF THE MASS.

The Sacrifice of the Altar one and the same with the Sacrifice of the Cross,—a continuation, a representation, and a commemoration thereof.

"In the Sacrifice of the Mass is contained, and "immolated, in an unbloody manner, the same Jesus "Christ who once offered Himself a bloody victim on "the altar of the Cross: in the Mass, the victim is the "same, and the principal Priest the same as on the "Cross; the only difference being in the mode of obla-"tion: the merits or fruits of the bloody Sacrifice of "the Cross, are abundantly imparted to our souls by "the unbloody Sacrifice of the Mass."
 (Council of Trent, Session 22, ch. 2.)

Public worship is a duty which we owe to God, and sacrifice the proper manner of fulfilling that duty, according to His will. It was God Himself that revealed to man this mode of worshiping Him. From the creation of the world, sacrifice has ever constituted the chief feature of that religion, which God gave to man.

It is emphatically the worship of God, the worship which God ordained to be rendered to Himself alone. Sacrifice and religion, sacrifice and Divine worship, are, in effect, one and the same thing. The abolition of Sacrifice would have been regarded as the extinction of all religion. Had sacrifice been abolished, the solemn worship of God would have been considered to have ceased throughout the world; God would no longer be looked upon as receiving the honour due to His name. Hence, the prophets, describing the extinction of religion, represent the people of God as "*sitting without sacrifice or altar,*" (Osee iii. 4.): "*and the continual sacrifice taken away.*" (Dan. xii. 11.)

Sacrifice was never to cease: Carnal sacrifices indeed, the sacrifices of bulls and goats, were to be done away; but another and a better sacrifice was to come in their stead. This, the prophets foretold in various ways. There was to be a sacrifice essentially pure and holy, which was to supersede all the carnal sacrifices that heretofore had been offered. It was to be celebrated everywhere throughout the world, among all nations: it was to go on continually, and was never to cease as long as the sun and moon should stand. All this I have shown in the preceding chapter.

Before entering upon the subject of the perpetual and universal Sacrifice of the Mass, it may be proper to remind the reader of four fundamental truths, that have an essential reference to this matter.

1st. It was through the disobedience of our first parents Adam and Eve, that sin and death entered the world; and that both sin and death passed upon all their descendants, they having sinned in the persons of their first parents; in punishment of which first sin, the gates of heaven were closed against the whole human race, they all being children of wrath. (Ephes. ii. 3.)

2nd. In fulfilment of the promise made to our first parents immediately after their fall—*that of the woman should be born one that should crush the head of the serpent*, (Genesis iii. 15.) the second Person of the adorable Trinity took upon Him our human nature, in order to *destroy the works of the devil*, (1 John iii. 8.) who had induced our first parents to transgress—to effect our reconciliation with heaven, and to restore us to our original condition; for unless He became man, He could not suffer; and unless He were God, He could not by His sufferings have effected our redemption; but being both God and man, He was capable of suffering, and His sufferings were effectual in redeeming us. "Hence," St. Paul says, "as by the offence of the first man (Adam), con-"demnation was brought upon all men; so, by "the justice of the Man-God, the justification of "life is brought within the reach of all men. As "by the disobedience of one man (Adam) all were "made sinners; so, by the obedience of one man (Christ) many are made just." (Rom. v. 18, 19.)

3rd. Christ by His death on the cross, has "delivered us from the power of darkness, and "transferred us into the kingdom of His Eternal "Father. He has reconciled all things in Himself, "making peace through the blood of His Cross, "both as to the things that are on earth, and the "things that are in heaven; blotting out the hand-"writing of the decree that stood against us, He "nailed it to the cross; and stripping the powers "and principalities of darkness of the power they "had over mankind, He confidently made a show "of them, openly triumphing over them in Him-"self." (Colos. i. 13, 20; ii. 14, 15.) Satan then ceased to be the prince of this world. (John xvi. 11.) Christ unlocked and threw open to mankind the gates of heaven, that had remained closed ever since the fall of Adam, during the space of four thousand years. "When Thou didst overcome the "sharpness of death, Thou didst open the king-"dom of heaven to all believers." (Te Deum.)

Not only did Christ, by the Sacrifice of the Cross, and by His other sufferings, pay the price of our redemption, He also thereby acquired an infinite treasure of merits, by which He purchased for us all spiritual benedictions and graces in this life, all the means necessary for obtaining eternal happiness, and eternal happiness itself in the life to come; insomuch, that it is only in, and through Him, that any grace or blessing is bestowed on us by God; or that anything we can do, can be agreeable or acceptable to Him. In a word, He not only prevented us from perishing everlastingly, by delivering us from the condemnation which we had incurred by the sin of our first parents, and by our own sins—He has moreover acquired infinite merits, by which He purchased for us eternal life, together with all the graces and helps necessary for us to obtain it. In a word, by the Sacrifice of the Cross, Christ delivered us from sin and hell, and purchased for us, mercy, grace, and salvation. In other words, the Son of God died for us; He made over to us the merits of His Passion and Death; He purchased for us those graces for which we pray; His blood continually pleads for us.

Nay, from the beginning of the world, the Passion of Christ has ever been the great object of the devotion of the children of God, who always celebrated it beforehand, and expressed their faith and confidence in it, by the offering up of bloody sacrifices of animals.

Hence, Christ is in Scripture, called "The Lamb slain from the commencement of the world." (Apocalypse xiii. 8.) The reason of this devotion to the future Sacrifice of the Cross is, that ever since the time of the fall of Adam, no grace could be derived to any man, but through the channel of the merits of the future passion and death of the Redeemer. If, then, through the means of bloody sacrifices of animals, the ancient just obtained a share in the future Sacrifice of the Cross, how much more now, since Christ has come into the world, and has offered Himself a victim on the Cross, by which He has reconciled us to Himself, is His Passion and Death the fountain of life and the source of all grace, and good to mankind.

The full effects of the Sacrifice of the Cross were, however, suspended till it had been actually offered up; and the souls of the ancient just, who, by believing in the future Redeemer, had obtained admission into Limbo, were detained there till their price of redemption had been actually paid.

During the four thousand years that preceded the oblation of the Victim of Calvary, all the great events that took place on the face of the earth, were but so many preparations for this greatest of all events. Empires and kingdoms rose and fell to prepare His way. When God appeared to the Patriarchs, it was to confirm them in the faith of the Redeemer to come. When He inspired the Prophets, it was to keep alive in His people this faith, by pointing out to them the circumstances of the time and place of His coming, and by portraying His features and future actions, that He might be the more easily recognised at His coming. The faith in the Redeemer to come was the chief article of belief of the people of God in those times. When He did come, the whole world was reduced under one government, and peace reigned throughout it, in order to facilitate the propagation of the benefits of His coming.

At last, in the fulness of time, the hour for the redemption of mankind, struck on the clock of eternity; immediately the Lamb of God, the august Victim, which had been long and so impatiently expected by angels and by men, descended from heaven upon earth to destroy the works of the devil. A new Victim is placed upon a new Altar: the Cross is the altar, not of one temple, but of the whole world, (S. Leo.) of all generations of mankind, past, present, and to come. The great sacrifice has been accomplished; we know the place, the day, and the hour thereof. It was at Jerusalem, on Mount Calvary, and under the canopy of heaven that it was offered up; *but its blood has bathed the whole world, (Origenes in Levit.)* At this sight, God and man, heaven and earth, angels and all creatures, were seized with grief and with joy; with grief for His sufferings, with joy for their happy effects. His blood has proved beneficial to all. It gave glory to God, and peace to mankind; for "it

"has pleased God to reconcile all things by Him,
"who is the Principle of life, and the firstborn from
"among the dead; making peace through the
"blood of His Cross, both as to the things that
"are on earth, and the things that are in heaven."
(Col. i. 18, 20.)

Now the Sacrifice of the Mass is the continuation, the real representation, and the commemoration of the great Sacrifice of the Cross.

1.—*The Sacrifice of the Mass is the continuation of the Sacrifice of the Cross.*

In order fully to partake of the benefits of a sacrifice, it is necessary to partake of the flesh of the victim of that sacrifice: in other words, communion is an essential part of sacrifice. Among all nations, both priests and peoples always partook of the flesh of the victim: it is an indispensable condition of sacrifice; a law revealed from the origin of the world; a condition imposed upon mankind by God Himself.

It has ever been the universal conviction of mankind, that, by partaking of the substances that had been immolated, they communed with the Divinity. Accordingly, St. Paul says, (1 Cor. x. 18.) "The Jews offer sacrifices; and to partake of
"those sacrifices is to be made partakers of the altar
"on which they are offered; to hold communion
"*with God; and to offer Him supreme worship.*"

"The heathens offer sacrifice to devils; and to eat "of those sacrifices is to be made partakers with "devils, and to hold communion with devils, nay, "to offer up supreme worship to devils." Therefore St. Paul forbade the Corinthians to eat of meats which they had reason to suspect had been offered up to idols; for, to partake of such meats, *would be to commit the crime of idolatry.* In like manner, in order to offer supreme worship to God, to commune with God, to participate in the merits of the Sacrifice of the Cross, the Sacrifice of the New Law must have a communion, and the flesh of the Victim thereof must be partaken of. As, therefore, the Sacrifice of the Cross is the sacrifice of all countries, of all ages, of the whole human race, there must be a means, by which all the successive generations of mankind may be enabled to partake thereof, until the end of time.

But, as Christ was to die but once, to suffer but once, to offer Himself, in a bloody manner, but once, to redeem us but once, to make atonement for sin and satisfaction to God's justice for us but once, how are we, who, for instance, live upwards of eighteen hundred years after the death of Christ, how are we to partake of the flesh of the Victim of the Sacrifice of the Cross? to receive any present benefit from His atonement? How is the Passion of Christ to be brought near to us, or we to it? It is not enough that the

Sacrifice of the Cross has been offered many years ago; its effects must be applied to our souls, that we may have a share in the redemption purchased for us. In a word, how are we to partake of the Victim of Calvary?

The Council of Trent explains this: "*The "almighty power and goodness of God,*" it says, "*has provided for this, by an incomprehensible "design, which surpasses our weak understand- "ings. He has perpetuated unto the end of the "world, this self-same great Sacrifice of Calvary, "once materially offered for the salvation of "mankind. Through His immense goodness, the "immolated flesh of the Victim of Calvary is "presented to us under the appearance of bread "and wine: and it is declared 'that whoever "refuses to partake thereof shall not have life in "him.*' (St. John vi. 54.) *For, our Lord, being "on the point of offering Himself a victim on the "Cross, for the redemption of mankind; as His "Priesthood was not to cease with His mortal "life, He, on the very night on which He was "betrayed, instituted and left to His Church a "visible and unbloody Sacrifice, by which the "bloody Sacrifice of the Cross, that could be "offered but once, might be perpetuated until the "end of time, and its salutary virtue and efficacy "communicated to all mankind, for the remission "of their sins. Declaring Himself a High Priest* "*for ever, according to the order of Melchisedech, He offered up to His Eternal Father the sacrifice of His Body and Blood under the appearance of bread and wine; and immediately distributed them to His apostles; constituting them, and their successors, His ministers, to continue to offer up the same Sacrifice unto the end of time, by saying, 'Do this in remembrance of Me.'*"—(Council of Trent, Sess. xxii. 1.)

What, therefore, was wanting to the Sacrifice of the Cross, is supplied at the altars of the Church. The Mass is, therefore, a continuation of the Sacrifice of the Cross, to enable us to partake of the great Victim of Calvary. Hence, the Mass is a true and real sacrifice, the same sacrifice as that of the Cross, from which it differs only as to the mode of oblation.

On the Cross, there were immolation and oblation; in the Mass, there is no immolation, but a second oblation of the Victim of the Cross. The same Victim which was once offered on the Cross, is again offered on our altars: but on the Cross, it was only offered up; while on our altars it is offered up and distributed.

The actual shedding of blood is not an essential part of sacrifice; for the same blood, once already offered up in sacrifice, may be again offered up, to constitute a second distinct sacrifice.

Thus, the Jewish High Priest, on the solemn festival of expiation, did not immolate a fresh victim within the Holy of Holies; but carried with him, within the veil, the blood of the victim, that had been previously shed on the outer altar of holocausts, and offered it up a second time *to accomplish atonement:* which second offering constituted of itself a sacrifice, although not accompanied with the shedding of blood.

In like manner, Jesus Christ does not die a second time on our altars. He does not perform again the Sacrifice of the Cross, so as to shed His blood and die afresh; but the sacrifice which, once for all, He offered on the Cross, He continually renews upon the altar. The Sacrifice of the Cross, and that of the Mass, are, therefore, one and the same Sacrifice. First offered in the institution of the Holy Eucharist, then consummated on the Cross, it is perpetuated before the mercy-seat in heaven, and on the altars of the Church on earth : offered daily, in successive acts, by priests continually succeeding one another, unto the end of time, it is still one sacrifice, even as Christ Himself, who offers it, is one. Christ is there present, the principal author and invisible worker, to Whom is subject all that He wills, and to Whose command everything is obedient. "The visible priest," says à Kempis, (book iv. 5,) "is but the minister of Christ, using

"the words of Christ, by the command and insti-
"tution of Christ." To show that it is in the
Name and Person of Christ that the visible priest
acts, he does not say: "This is the body and
"blood of Christ," but, "This is My Body and
"Blood." The secondary priest wholly disappears, that Christ, the principal priest, may convert the bread and wine into His own Body and Blood.

Accordingly, à Kempis says: (book iv. 2,)
"As often as we repeat this mystery and receive
"the Body of Christ, so often is the Sacrifice of
"the Cross renewed, and we are made partakers
"of the merits of Christ's passion and death;
"for the charity of Christ is never diminished,
"nor is the greatness of His propitiation ever
"exhausted. As often, therefore, as we assist at
"the Mass, it ought to appear to us as great,
"new, and delightful, as if Christ, that same day,
"first descending into the Virgin's womb, had
"been made man; or, that hanging on the Cross,
"He was suffering and dying for the sins of the
"world."

Hence, the Mass is indispensably necessary in the economy of our sanctification and salvation; for, although the Sacrifice of the Cross made full satisfaction for our sins and paid our debts; yet the Mass is necessary, for the Sacrifice of Calvary must be consummated in us, that we may derive benefit from it; its fruits must be applied to our souls; in a word, we must partake of the great Victim of Calvary. The Divine Victim could not, in His natural state, be partaken of by the faithful; what then was wanting to the Sacrifice of the Cross is, by the Holy Communion, supplied at the altars of the Church. The Sacrifice of the Cross is accomplished and perfected on the altars of the Church, where Christ daily nourishes us with the sacrament of His passion. The Sacrifice of the Cross paid our ransom; the Sacrifice of the Mass imparts to each individual a share in this payment. Thus, the Sacrifice of the Cross becomes to us, not a mere event in history, which took place more than eighteen hundred years ago, but a present reality. The sacrifice of the great Victim commenced on Calvary, but did not end there: it commenced there, in order to continue till the end of time. It is consummated in the midst of us, without the shedding of blood. It is commemorated continually, but so commemorated as to be really that which, after an unbloody manner, is commemorated.

The Sacrifice of the Cross was of infinite value; its efficacy endures throughout all ages; its effects can never be exhausted. Hence à Kempis says: "The charity of Christ is never diminished, nor "the greatness of His propitiation ever exhausted." Each successive generation of mankind, as they appear upon the stage of this world, find the Divine banquet prepared, and are sanctified by incorporating the flesh and blood of the Victim of Calvary, the only universal and eternal Victim of heaven and earth; they thus obtain a share in the great Sacrifice of the Cross. Jesus Christ, our Redeemer, who is both our High Priest and Victim, who, to effect the work of our redemption, and reconcile us with our offended Creator, offered Himself once in a bloody manner upon the Cross, continues to offer Himself daily upon our altars in the Mass in an unbloody manner, by the ministry of His priests, in order to communicate and apply to our souls the fruits of His death.

So far, then, from the Sacrifice of the Altar arguing, as Protestants suppose, any insufficiency in the Sacrifice of the Cross, it, on the contrary, demonstrates the Sacrifice of the Cross to be of infinite value and of inexhaustible virtue; being capable of being continually drawn upon, daily renewed on millions of altars, and applied for the remission of the sins of all mankind, and for the sanctification of their souls.

2.—*The Mass is a real representation of the Passion and Death of Christ.*

The Passion and Death of Christ are, in a lively manner, represented to us, and all the mysteries of our redemption are solemnly celebrated by the separate consecration of the bread and wine, into the Body and Blood of Christ, the true Lamb of God, who takes away the sins of the world. He then and there presents Himself upon our altars, under the figure of death, that is, under the sacramental veils which represent His Body as delivered up, broken, and slain for us, and His Blood as shed for us; for the outward appearance of bread more naturally represents His Body; and the outward appearance of wine more naturally represents His Blood: these being separately consecrated, and lying separate on the altar, represent the real separation of His Blood from His Body, which took place when He actually died on the Cross. By this means, our holy Victim is offered up to God, *not actually dead,* but under the appearances of death. "I saw," says St. John, (Apoc. v. 6,) "and behold, in the midst of the "throne, of the four living creatures, and of "the ancients, a Lamb standing as it were "slain;" not actually slain, but *as it were slain,* under the appearance of being slain. Thus the whole Passion and Death of Christ are solemnly acted, as a most sacred tragedy by Himself in person; here that death, which is the fountain of all our good, is shown forth in such a manner as not only to be kept in our remembrance, but also to live in us, and bring forth in us the fruit of life: here the Blood of Christ most powerfully pleads and intercedes for us. Here, in fine, not only the Passion and Death, but also the victorious Resurrection, and triumphant Ascension of our crucified King, are solemnly commemorated.

3.—*The Mass is a commemoration of the Sacrifice of the Cross; yet so as to be really that which is commemorated.*

For this end did Christ institute the Eucharistic Sacrifice and Sacrament, and leave us therein the sacred mysteries of His Body and Blood, that we might always have before our eyes His Passion and Death, in order to oblige us to a perpetual gratitude for the great mystery of our redemption.

Accordingly, it is as an everlasting memorial of His Passion and Death that we frequent the holy Mass. Jesus Christ knew that He was liable to be forgotten by men, or at least to be but coldly remembered and loved by them, as years rolled on: He therefore contrived a means, by which to live amongst us to the end of time, and communicate to us the merits of His Passion and Death; by veiling both His Divinity and Humanity from the eyes of our senses, by the same Almighty power by which He had veiled His Divinity, whilst living amongst us upon earth. For, immediately after having instituted the holy Sacrifice, He said to His disciples; "*Do this in remembrance of Me;*" that is, continue to offer up, to partake of, and distribute this My Body and Blood, as a memorial of My death upon the Cross, that you may obtain everlasting salvation. St. Paul proclaims this same command to all generations of mankind: "As "often," says he, "as you shall eat of this Bread, "and drink of this Chalice, you shall always "remember that Christ died for you:" for, "there "is no other name under heaven, by which we "can be saved." (1 Cor. xi. 26.) Moreover, Christ's death upon the Cross, being the fountain of life, and the source of all grace to mankind, all the merits thereof would be lost to them, unless they kept up the memory of it in their minds, by continually commemorating it, and appropriating to themselves the merits thereof, by the continual offering up of the Sacrifice of the Mass. For, how could they believe in Him, hope in Him, love Him, and be saved by Him of whom they had lost sight, whom they had forgotten, of whom they had never heard, and on whom, consequently, they could not call? It was when about to deprive them of His visible presence, that He instituted this Sacrifice, and commanded it to be continually offered up, lest that they should ever forget Him, and all He did for them. He did not wish that there should be any other pledge than His own divine presence in the Eucharist, to keep alive the remembrance of Him. Each time, therefore, that we are present at the Mass, we should assist thereat, as we would have waited upon Him at the Sacrifice of Calvary itself, had we been there with a true belief in Him.

It is because Christ loves us, and desires to be loved by us, that He wishes to be remembered by us, in order to impart to us His merits. The remembrance of a person is a kind of presence which is dear to love; it is while bleeding and dying for us, while offering up for us the sacrifice of our redemption, that He particularly wishes to be remembered by us; for it is then that He most effectually shows how much He loves us, and desires to be loved by us. How, indeed, can we remember all the torments that He endured in order to open heaven for us, and to merit for us the graces necessary to enable us to arrive thither, without being convinced how sincerely He loves us and wishes to be loved by us? The numerous wounds, with which His body was covered, are so many eloquent tongues, that proclaim His love for us; and can a Christian be thoroughly persuaded of this His love for us, without at least desiring to make Him a return of love? It is difficult to decide which is the more criminal, to disbelieve Christ's presence in the Eucharistic Sacrifice, or, while believing it, not to love Him: hence St. Paul says, (1 Cor. xvi. 22,) "If any one love not our Lord Jesus Christ, "let him be accursed."

That we may the better understand the nature of the Sacrifice of the Mass, it is necessary to point out wherein it differs from the Sacrifice of the Cross.

1st. By the Sacrifice of the Cross, Christ redeemed the world. He then and there paid its redemption price, in His mangled flesh and streaming blood, and in the agonies of His Human Heart. He really suffered for us; He really died for us; His sufferings and death satisfied the divine justice, and merited for us the pardon and remission of our sins. He paid a full price for us; He made a perfect satisfaction for us; He wrought our eternal redemption. Nothing was wanting to His Sacrifice. It was infinite in value, and exhaustless in virtue; and is now the source of all grace, and the cause of our salvation.

It is not thus with the Sacrifice of the Mass. All its virtue flows from the Sacrifice of the Cross. All its value consists in coming after that

Sacrifice, in being commemorative of it, and in a manner renewing it—renewing in an unbloody manner, and without suffering, on the altar, what was done with blood and suffering upon the Cross; whatever force, then, the Sacrifice of the Mass has, comes from the Sacrifice offered on Calvary.

The second great difference between the Sacrifice of the Cross, and that of the Mass is, that the latter even though filled with virtue flowing from the Cross, is not properly either satisfactory or propitiatory. For when Christ offered Himself a Victim on the Cross, He was a *mortal* man. His acts were therefore both meritorious and satisfactory; but now He is *immortal*, and though really present on the altar, and Himself really the Victim that is sacrificed, yet such act is neither meritorious nor satisfactory; because being immortal and now incapable of suffering, He can no longer merit or make satisfaction for-sin. But in another sense the Mass is *propitiatory*. It begs and implores, through the merits of the Sacrifice of the Cross, the remission of sin for the whole world, or for those in whose special behalf it is offered. It is also, for the same reason, satisfactory, because it begs or implores the remission of the punishment of sin. All this it does, for the sake of that pure Victim which was offered bleeding on the Cross, and which is continually offered without blood upon the altar. When the priest, acting as minister of Christ, offers the most holy Sacrifice of the Mass, he performs the highest possible act of worship—he makes the most powerful act of supplication; for it is our great High Priest that is offering Himself; it is the "Minister of the true tabernacle" that is ministering for us; it is our Divine Intercessor interceding for us, the one Mediator between God and man. The Sacrifice of the altar is one way in which Christ fulfils for us His office of Intercessor. In a word, the Sacrifice of the Altar differs from the Sacrifice of the Cross, just so far, and in such sense, as the office which our Lord performs for us in His glorious life in heaven, differs from the office which He performed for us during His suffering life on earth. Both are portions of His mediatorial work. Once He offered Himself with suffering: now He offers Himself without suffering. On the Cross He redeemed us with His Blood: on the altar, He intercedes that we may individually have part in that redemption.

The third great difference is, that the Sacrifice of the Cross did but intercede; it did not *bestow* upon mankind the pardon which it purchased for them; otherwise all men would from that moment have been pardoned, justified, and saved. —Christ has paid the price of our redemption; but for individuals to benefit by what He has done, something more is necessary on their part; and in order that they may do this something, Christ does not withhold His graces. Those graces He bestows in many ways, especially by the sacraments. But the *Sacrifice* of the Mass is not a *sacrament;* it does not therefore *bestow* remission of sins; it does but ask and implore it; it pleads most powerfully for the sinner, that he may be brought to repentance, may make an act of true contrition, and obtain the remission of his sins. In this sense the Sacrifice of the Mass is a propitiatory Sacrifice.

If we would appease the anger of God, and deprecate His vengeance; if we would beg His mercy for ourselves or others, how can we more surely move Him to pity, than by representing before Him the Death and Passion of His beloved Son? But the Sacrifice of the Mass is no mere representation of that of the Cross; it does not merely commemorate the death of Christ, or remind the Eternal Father of it, as of a thing that happened many hundred years ago: it exhibits it before Him; it renews it, not merely in figure, but really and truly, though after an unbloody manner. Christ therein re-enacts, as in a mystery, the sacrifice of Himself, presents Himself upon the altar a Lamb, as it were slain, and makes propitiation for us.

PRAYER.

I believe, O Lord, help my unbelief; increase my faith, my Lord and my God : deliver me from all disbelief, from all torpor and dulness of faith, and from all indifference to this great mystery. Illuminate my understanding, that I may behold it in its proper light; strengthen me to believe it with an undoubted faith; for it is Thy work, not the power of man, Thy sacred institution, not man's invention.

Since the angels that surround the throne of God in heaven, descend upon earth and prostrate themselves before our altars, during the Sacred Mysteries, through respect for the Victim which is there immolated, with what sentiments of reverence should we assist thereat, we who are but dust and ashes, and whom sin has reduced to the lowest degree of misery? Illuminate, therefore, O God, our minds, that we may behold this mystery of God in the light of God; open our eyes, enliven our faith, as to the incomprehensible greatness of this sacred mystery; that, like the heavenly spirits, we may assist thereat with the same profound respect, as if we were in company with them before the throne of God's glory in heaven. Amen.

CHAPTER IV.

THE SACRIFICE OF THE MASS A TRUE AND PROPER SACRIFICE.

" In every place there is offered to My Name a clean "oblation." (Malachi i. 11.)

"This is My Body, which is broken, which is given "for you. This is the chalice of the New Testament, in "My Blood, which is, which shall be, shed for many "unto the remission of sins." (St. Matt. xxvi. 26, 28; 1 Cor. xi. 24.)

Protestantism has taken upon itself to abolish the great Christian sacrifice. It has done away with that which everywhere, and by all Christians throughout the whole world, has ever been regarded as the highest and most essential act of Divine worship. It is of the utmost consequence that the nature of this tremendous change should be fully understood; for it is a principal difference between Protestantism and the Catholic Church, that Protestantism has rejected, and the Catholic Church retained, the holy Sacrifice of the Mass. In punishment of their sins, strength was given to Satan against the perpetual Sacrifice. (Daniel viii. 12.)

We must always bear in mind that the Eucha-,

rist is both a sacrifice and a sacrament; its object, as a sacrifice, is principally to worship God; and, as a sacrament, to bestow grace on our souls. As a sacrifice, the Mass is available to all who join in offering it up, or for whom, though absent, it is offered up. As a sacrament, it is available to those only who partake of the altar. Thus, to the priest it is always available, both as a sacrifice and a sacrament, because he offers it up and consumes it. To those who assist thereat, it is always available as a sacrifice; but as a sacrament, it is only available to those who communicate.

It is here question of the Mass only as a Sacrifice.

I explained the nature of the Sacrifice of the Mass above; I showed it to be the channel through which the merits of the Sacrifice of the Cross flow into our souls. *I now proceed* to show "that the Mass is itself a true and proper Sacrifice," not merely a religious rite or ceremony representing the Sacrifice of Calvary, but a true, real, and unbloody, sacrifice; for Jesus Christ, our Redeemer, who is both our High Priest and Victim, and who, to perfect the work of our redemption, and reconcile man with his offended Creator, once offered Himself in a bloody manner upon the Cross, in order to communicate and apply to our souls the fruits of His Passion and Death,— communicates Himself daily, in an unbloody manner, upon our altars in the Mass, by the ministry of His priests.

I have shown above, from the words of Christ, and of the prophets, that a pure and holy sacrifice was to supersede the Jewish sacrifices; that it was to be everywhere celebrated throughout the world, and never to cease, as long as the sun and moon shall last. Now this sacrifice can be no other than that of the Holy Mass; for it is a pure sacrifice, and is universal as to both time and place. It is the chief and principal worship of the Catholic Church, which is the only religion that extends from the rising to the setting of the sun.

The Mass is retained and offered up by the Greek and Oriental Churches and sects. No other sacrifice is offered up anywhere. Therefore, as sacrifice is never to cease until the end of the world, and as the Mass is the only sacrifice everywhere offered up throughout the world, it must be the sacrifice foretold by Christ, and by the prophets, and which is to last for ever.

We read in the twenty-fourth chapter of Exodus, that, immediately after the promulgation of the law on Mount Sinai, Moses, in accordance with the command of God, had committed to writing the law, he ordered a sacrifice to be " offered up; and, " having read the words of the covenant in the " hearing of the people, he took the blood of the " victim, and therewith sprinkled both them and "the book of the law, saying, *This is the blood of the covenant which the Lord hath made with you.*" He thus executed God's covenant with the children of Israel. In like manner our Blessed Lord, at the close of His mortal life, sealed the new covenant: for, taking the chalice, He gave it to His apostles, saying, "*Drink ye all of this; for this is the Blood of the New Testament, or covenant.*" "*Do this in remembrance of Me.*" Now, as the blood, with which Moses sprinkled the people, was the blood of a victim, already sacrificed; so also the blood which our Lord gave to His apostles to drink was also the blood of a sacrifice; that is to say, our Blessed Lord offered Himself up in sacrifice, before giving His blood to His disciples to drink, saying: "*Drink ye all of this;*" "*Do this in remembrance of Me.*" He there and then sealed and executed, with His blood the new and eternal covenant, and all its promises, to mankind, and afterwards confirmed it by His death on the Cross.

In the words of the institution of the Eucharist, Christ says, "This is My Body which *is* given *for you;* This is My Blood which *is* shed *for you.*" The shedding of the Blood, and the giving and the breaking of the Body, are here a present thing, which takes place while the words are spoken; therefore a sacrifice was there and then instituted and offered up.

The use of the word "*broken*" and of those others, *of the bread which we break*, shows that it is the Eucharistic bread, or the body of Christ, under the appearance of bread, which is spoken of by St. Paul; for on the Cross the body of Christ was not broken, and as bread only, could it be broken.

Observe, moreover, that the body of Christ is here said to be *broken* and *given for you;* that is, *not only to be eaten by you as a sacrament; but offered in sacrifice to God for you.*

Also, it is not of His blood, as shed on the Cross, but as *poured out from the chalice or cup,* that St. Paul speaks.

St. Paul says, (1 Cor. x. 16,) "The chalice of "benediction, which we bless, *is it not the com-* "*munion of the blood of Christ?* and the bread "which we break, *is it not the partaking of the* "*body of the Lord?*" The apostle here makes use of the interrogative form of speech; which proves that he meant and taught the mystery of the real presence of Christ in the Eucharist; for this form of speech is never used, but when the truth in question is equally admitted by him who speaks, as well as by those to whom he speaks. Is it not, says the apostle, the participation of the Body and Blood of Christ? Is it not one of the mysteries, revealed to me from above, which I have always taught both you and all nations? is it not a principal mystery of our common faith?

Our Lord concluded the words of the institution of the Eucharist by saying, "*Do this in "remembrance of Me;*" that is, I hereby authorize and command you to offer up, to partake of, and distribute My Body and Blood, as a memorial of My Passion and Death, *In remembrance, or for a commemoration of Me.* These words perfectly express the Catholic doctrine; for the Sacrifice of the Mass is a Sacrifice, commemorative of the Sacrifice of the Cross.

The Mosaic sacrifices represented the Sacrifice of the Cross as *future*, the Sacrifice of the Mass represents it as *past;* as, therefore, the Mosaic sacrifices, although only representative of a future Sacrifice, were true and real sacrifices; so the Sacrifice of the Mass, which is commemorative of a past Sacrifice, is also a true and real sacrifice.

What our Lord bade the apostles to do, we find them actually *doing.* Thus, in the Book of their Acts, (Acts ii. 46,) we find them *continuing in the communication of the breaking of bread—and in the breaking of bread from house to house:* for as yet they had no public church of their own. Again, when it is said, in the thirteenth chapter of the Acts, that certain prophets and doctors were *ministering to the Lord,* the word ministering, in the original Greek, properly denotes the offering up of sacrifice, in the solemn ministration of the Church.

I will not dwell further on texts of Scripture, to prove the Mass to be a sacrifice; for, it is both the *written* and *unwritten* word of God conjointly, as interpreted by the lawful successors of the apostles, the bishops of the true Church of Christ, and not the private interpretation by every individual, of the written word alone, that is the rule of faith, left us by Christ. To require, then, of a Catholic, to quote chapter and verse, in proof of the Mass being a sacrifice, as if that kind of proof were necessary to his position, would be to endeavour to make him establish the Catholic faith on Protestant grounds. The New Testament was never intended to teach us, for the first time, what Christ had done and said. All this had been committed to writing, and, what is more, observed by the Church, long before any of the Gospels had been written, and several hundred years before the books of the New Testament were collected into their present form. "From the dawn of Chris-
" tianity, the Church has ever invariably been the
" teacher of the doctrine of Christ. The Church
" is the rule, appointed by Jesus Christ, by which
" we are to come to the knowledge of all the
" truths of revelation, of the inspiration of the
" Scriptures, and of the true sense and meaning
" of them. The Church is the organ of God, by

"which He speaks to mankind, and discovers to
"them the truths of eternity. She is the chan-
"nel by which all revealed truths are transmitted
"to them." In accordance with this divine rule,
the lawful successors of the apostles, the bishops
of Christendom, assembled at Trent in the year
A.D. 1563, having clear and full evidence of
what was then, and had always been, the unanimous doctrine of the Universal Church concerning the Holy Mass, pronounced it to *be a
true and proper sacrifice.* (Sess. xxii.) Hence
the Mass has ever, since the origin of Christianity, been believed to be a Sacrifice, and offered
up as such; for the Church never changes her
faith, nor allows any one in her communion to
change or even question any one article of it.
Like her divine Founder, her doctrine *is yesterday,
and to-day, and the same for ever.* (Heb. xiii. 8.)
The doctrine of the Sacrifice of the Mass is, therefore, an important portion of the "faith once
"delivered to the saints," (Jude 3) which the
Church of God has ever guarded and preserved as
the apple of her eye.

The declaration made at Trent, of the Mass
being a true and proper Sacrifice, was not the decision of a few individuals, but the unanimous doctrine of the great body of the first pastors of the
Christian Church, spread over the face of the earth;
for the two hundred and fifty bishops assembled

there were but the delegates and representatives of all the Bishops of Christendom, by whom the Tridentine decrees were accepted and confirmed; their decision bears the signature and seal of the successor of St. Peter. As those bishops differed in country, language, manners, government, worldly interests, and even in opinions concerning matters of knowledge and learning, when we behold them perfectly unanimous in so important and delicate a matter, as that of religion, are we not forced to exclaim, *The finger of God is here!* What but the overruling providence of God could keep perfectly united, in one religion, a multitude of persons of all nations, who disagreed in almost every other respect? Is it not safer to prefer their unanimous decision in declaring the Mass to be a true and proper Sacrifice, to trusting to one's own private judgment, in opposition to them? Among those who do not follow this rule, scarcely are two persons to be found, of the same nation and language, nay, of the same family, who perfectly agree on any one article of religion.

The body of the first pastors of the Church, in pronouncing the Mass to be a Sacrifice, solemnly declared and protested it to be the original doctrine, without addition or diminution, which had been handed down to them from the Apostles. They all proclaimed: "*So have we received; so the* "*universal Church has ever believed; let there,* "*then, be no new doctrine admitted; none, but* "*what has been handed down to us from the* "*apostles.*" "*Such is the true meaning of the* "*words of Christ; such is the meaning taught* "*by the apostles throughout the world, and* "*handed down to us through the divinely ap-* "*pointed channel of an universal and uninter-* "*rupted tradition.*" This doctrine has always been believed everywhere and by all.

Tradition is the rule, laid down by Christ, and promulgated throughout the world by His inspired apostles, for the preservation and perpetuation, in their purity, of all His revealed truths, till the end of time. Now, tradition consists, in handing down, from generation to generation, by word of mouth, or by writing, the true interpretation and meaning of the sacred Scriptures, and all the truths revealed by Christ to His apostles, which are not contained in them. The principle upon which the rule of tradition is founded is—firmly and invariably to embrace and adopt in every generation, the doctrine received from the preceding generation, and carefully to transmit the same to the succeeding generation, without addition or diminution. This principle of tradition was established by the inspired apostles, as the means for perpetuating all divine truths, and as a barrier to prevent innovation.

To confine myself to one proof, St. Paul thus writes to St. Timothy, (2 Tim. ii. 2.) *"The things " thou hast heard from me, before many witnesses, " the same commit to faithful men, who shall be fit " to teach them to others."* And iii. 14, *" Con-" tinue in those things which thou hast learned " from me, and which have been communicated to " thee, knowing of whom thou hast learned " them."* Thus the Bishops, the chief pastors of the Church, are particularly charged with the obligation of adhering to the doctrine received from their predecessors, and of transmitting them to their successors. St. Augustine, in the fifth century of Christianity, bears testimony to the fidelity with which this rule was observed in his own, and in the preceding ages. *" Quod " invenerunt in ecclesia, tenuerunt, quod didice-" runt, docuerunt, quod a patribus acceperunt, " filiis tradiderunt."* (St. Aug. l. 2, contra Faustum, c. 10.) The bishops have, in all ages, held fast the doctrines which they found in the Church; they taught no others. They handed down to their successors all the identical doctrines they had received from their predecessors. This is the channel through which all Christian truths and mysteries, and, among others, that of the Sacrifice of the Mass, have been handed down to us from Christ and the apostles. No doctrine is to be held but what dates from the time of the apostles.

Since, then, the pastors of the second age of Christianity believed and taught as divine truths those doctrines only which they had learned from the apostles, and from those appointed by them personally, the faith of the first age of Christianity was necessarily the same as that which the Bishops of the second age delivered entire and uncorrupted to the Bishops of the third age; and the faith of the third age, was therefore necessarily the same as that of the two preceding ages. The same rule has been observed in every succeeding age, till the present day, and will continue to be so to the end of the world.

Such is the channel by which the faith of the Sacrifice of the Mass has been transmitted to us from Christ and the apostles.

But what crowns, and carries to the highest degree of certitude, the decision of the Church at Trent, declaring the Mass to be a true and proper Sacrifice, is the promise of infallibility made by the Holy Ghost to the Church, and confirmed by Christ: "*That the words once put into her "mouth shall never depart out of it; nor out of "the mouth of her seed, nor out of the mouth of "her seed's seed, from henceforth and for ever.*" (Isaias lix.) The seed or posterity of the Redeemer is the Church; the Holy Ghost here promises that the true meaning of revealed truths shall never cease to be held and taught by the Church. This divine promise is renewed and confirmed by Christ: *"When,"* says He, *"the Spirit of Truth shall come, He will teach you all truth, and abide with you for ever."* (St. John xvi. 13, and xiv. 16.) *"Go,"* says He, *"and teach all nations;"* behold, *"I am with you all days, even to the end of the world."* (St. Mat. xxviii. 20.) If, then, Christ Himself is to be with the successors of the apostles till the end of time, to assist them in teaching the nations of the earth; if the Holy Ghost is to descend upon them, and to abide with them for ever, to enable them to teach all truths, how can they teach error? If the inspiration of Christ and of the Holy Ghost, does not preserve them from error, what will? If the above words do not contain the promise of infallibility, they have no meaning whatever.

A further proof of the divine origin of the faith of the Sacrifice of the Mass, is found in the liturgies of the primitive ages of Christianity. A liturgy is the collection of prayers, by which the Christian public worship is performed.

Now, all the Liturgies of those countries in which Christianity was established by the apostles personally, and which were composed while the doctrine of the Catholic Church is acknowledged, even by Protestants, to have been pure, contain in the most expressive language the doctrine of the Sacrifice of the Mass. For in all these Liturgies, we find prayers corresponding with the principal parts of the Sacrifice, as, the prayers preparatory to it, the prayer of the invocation, of the oblation, of the communion, and of the thanksgiving. The first Liturgy was, in accordance with the teaching of Christ, drawn up by the apostles at Jerusalem, on Pentecost, immediately after the descent of the Holy Ghost; it was not committed to writing, but intrusted to the memory of the inspired apostles. St. James Major, who ruled the Church of Jerusalem during twenty-nine years, invariably administered the Holy Eucharist according to the form agreed upon between the other apostles and himself; the other apostles taught this Liturgy to the bishops and priests whom they ordained, and established it in all the churches they founded throughout the Roman Empire. The Liturgies frequently served as a creed; and any doctrine not conformable with them was immediately rejected with horror. Hence the axiom: the form of prayer is the rule of faith. "*Lex orandi, lex credendi.*" During the first four centuries of Christianity, the Liturgies were not committed to writing, but continued to be intrusted to the memory of the bishops and priests; "mysteria chartis non committenda; sit memoria "vobis codex:" for so astounding to the ears of the heathens, would the Christian mysteries have sounded, that they would have created in their minds an invincible prejudice against the Christian religion itself. The mysteries were the last thing taught to catechumens, immediately before baptism, when their minds and hearts were, by previous instruction, duly prepared to believe and reverence them.

It was not till the year A.D. 431, while assembled at the General Council of Ephesus, that the Bishops of Christendom came to the resolution of committing to writing the Liturgies of all the different Churches, as the reasons which had hitherto prevented their publication no longer existed, and as there then existed other stronger reasons, why they should no longer be intrusted solely to the memories of the bishops and priests. When, then, the Liturgies appeared in writing, they were all found perfectly to agree with each other in essentials. The meaning of the prayers that preceded, accompanied, and followed the Eucharistic Consecration was identical in them all.

They clearly expressed, the unbloody Sacrifice, the Victim, the invocation, the oblation, the change of substance, the real Presence, and adoration. Those Liturgies were substantially identical with the original Liturgy drawn up at Jerusalem, immediately after Pentecost; they all denoted a common origin; they all bore, in their principal features, a perfect resemblance, and, if I may use the expression, a family likeness.

If, then, notwithstanding the changes to which the original Liturgy, composed at Jerusalem, was exposed, during 431 years, from having been translated into the languages of all the different nations that composed the Roman Empire, yet, on these Liturgies being committed to writing, they were all found clearly to express the faith of the Sacrifice of the Mass, this uniformity must have proceeded from its divine and apostolical origin. Could any other cause have united all the national Churches of the world in precisely the same faith, and in the scrupulous profession of it, under the most trying circumstances?

Moreover, the faith of the Sacrifice of the Mass is not peculiar to the Catholic Church: it is also professed by all the Greek and Oriental Churches, and by the different sects that have, from time to time, separated from them; insomuch that the faith of the Sacrifice of the Mass is unanimously professed by all Christian nations whatever, with the exception of the comparatively few who inhabit the northern parts of Europe. The Greek schism, which commenced A.D. 891, was finally consummated shortly after the Council of Florence, in 1439; since then the Greek

Church has ever remained separate from the Catholic Church. Some of the Greek and Eastern sects had separated from the Greek Church in the fourth and fifth centuries. At the present day, we distinguish in the East, the Melchite, or common Greeks of Turkey, the Armenians, the Jacobites, the Christians of St. Thomas in India, the Copts, and the Ethiopians in Africa, all of whom have different Liturgies; yet they all offer up the Mass, as a Sacrifice, with as much firmness of faith as we Catholics do. There are, under the Russian and Ottoman sceptres, upwards of sixty millions of persons belonging to the Greek Church, all of whom profess the Mass to be a sacrifice. As all those churches and sects have been totally separated from the Catholic Church, some eight hundred and ninety years, and others fourteen hundred years, it is impossible that they should have derived any doctrines or practices from the Catholic Church since the time of their separation from it; and divided, as they have been, among themselves, they cannot have combined to adopt the doctrine of the Sacrifice of the Mass. On the other hand, since the rise of Protestantism, several attempts have been made, by the Lutherans of Germany, and by the Calvinists of Holland, to draw some or other of the Oriental Churches over to their novel creeds; but all in vain. Councils were held at Constantinople and in Palestine to protest against all those innovations. Anathemas were pronounced against all who denied the existence of Purgatory, of the seven sacraments, and of the Mass, as a sacrifice. The institution of the apostles, and their authority, which is equally sacred, in the eyes both of Catholics and of all ancient heretics and schismatics, can alone assign a sufficient reason for so perfect a uniformity among them, on the subject of the Sacrifice of the Mass. That not only do the original orthodox Liturgies, but also those of the most ancient heretical and schismatical sects, perfectly agree in the prayers that precede, accompany, and follow the consecration, and that they all express, in the clearest and most energetic terms, the belief of the existence of the Sacrifice of the Mass, of the real Presence, of Transubstantiation, and adoration, is satisfactorily proved, by the following extracts from their respective Liturgies.

1. As to the Liturgies of the Western Church. In the ancient Latin Liturgy, drawn up by Pope Gelasius, A.D. 450, and introduced into the British Isles, A.D. 595, at the time of the conversion of the Anglo-Saxons to Christianity, which for many centuries has been in use in France, Germany, and Spain, and which is still the Liturgy of the whole Western or Latin Church, we read the following invocation: " In compliance

" with the command of our Saviour, we offer to
" Thee, O God, this bread and this chalice, giving
" Thee thanks for allowing us to exercise the
" *priesthood* in Thy Presence. We beseech Thee
" to accept these *offerings*, made in honour of
" Christ; and to send down on this *Sacrifice* the
" Holy Ghost, that the bread *may become the Body,
" and the wine, the Blood of Christ.*" After the
consecration we read: " We offer to Thy Supreme
" Majesty, this pure *Host,* this *Holy Host,* this
" spotless *Host.*" The words, *oblation, offering,*
and *Host,* are here synonymous with the word
" sacrifice."

In the abridgment of the Liturgy introduced
into the primitive Christian Churches of Roman
Gaul, by SS. Irenæus and Photinus, and preserved
among the writings of St. Gregory of Tours, we
read the following extract : " The oblation is con-
" secrated on the patena. The angel of God
" descends on the *altar,* as it did on Christ's
" monument, at His resurrection, and blesses the
" *Host;* the clergy, in a suppliant attitude, pre-
" viously sing this anthem : We humbly entreat
" Thee, O God, to accept, bless, and sanctify
" *this Sacrifice,* that it may become for us *the
" Body and Blood of Christ.* May the Holy
" Ghost, Thy eternal co-operator, descend on this
" Sacrifice, that this bread and wine, being
" changed into the Body and Blood of Christ,

"which we here offer for our sins, may save us by "their merits."

In the Gallico-Gothic Liturgy, of the seventh century, we read the following prayer, preparatory to communion: "Fulfilling the sacred solemni- "ties, according to the rite of the *High Priest* "*Melchisedech*, we entreat of Thee, O God, the "grace worthily to receive the bread changed into "the Body of Christ, and to drink out of the "chalice, *the same Blood that flowed from* "*Christ's side on the Cross.*" To make an offering, according to the rite of the High Priest, Melchisedech, undoubtedly means to offer up sacrifice.

I now come to the original Greek and Oriental Liturgies, genuine copies of which are preserved in the French Imperial Library, Richelieu Street, Paris. In the year 1670, Colbert, the great Prime Minister of State, of Louis XIV., King of France, sent to the East to collect Greek and Oriental manuscripts of all kinds, Vansleb, a German Lutheran, thoroughly versed in the Greek and Oriental languages. After having travelled through the whole of the Levant, and visited particularly all the ancient monasteries, which were the principal depots of ancient lore, this intelligent and indefatigable traveller returned to France, with five hundred manuscripts of all sorts, among which are copies of all the original

Christian Liturgies of the different churches. From this source did Nicole, Renaudot, Lebrun, Treverne, and other champions and defenders of the Catholic faith, draw their invincible proofs of the divine and apostolical origin of all the Catholic doctrines, rejected by Protestantism.

In the Liturgy of St. John of Jerusalem we read the following offertory: "*We offer to Thee,* "*O God, this redoubtable and unbloody Sacri-* "*fice.*" In the Liturgy of Constantinople, first called that of the apostles, and afterwards that of St. Chrysostom, we read the following offertory: "Receive us, O Lord, at Thy *altar*, according to "Thy great mercy, that we may be worthy to "offer to Thee this *reasonable* and *unbloody* "*Sacrifice* for our sins, and for the ignorances of "the people." Having pronounced the words of the institution of the Eucharist, (which are not omitted in any of the Liturgies,) the priest, bowing down, secretly says: "We offer to Thee, O "God, this *reasonable* and *unbloody* sacrifice, and "entreat Thee to *change the bread into the pre-* "*cious Body of Christ, and the wine into His* "*precious Blood.*" The Liturgy of Constantinople, from which the above extract is taken, is that made use of by all the Greeks resident in the West, the Mingrelians and Georgians, the Bulgarians, Muscovites, and other Russians, and the modern Christian Melchites, and by all those who recognize the authority of the Greek Schismatic Patriarchs of Alexandria, Jerusalem, and Antioch.

In the Liturgy of Alexandria, composed by the Evangelist St. Mark, and also called that of St. Cyril, we read the following preparatory prayer: "By the power of the Holy Spirit, render us "worthy to offer up to Thee *this sacrifice of bene-* "*diction.*" At the approach of the Holy Communion, the priest makes the following act of faith: "I believe, and I will believe, to the last "breath of my life, that this is the life-giving "Body of our Lord and Saviour Jesus Christ, "which He assumed of the Virgin Mary." He "bore a good testimony before Pontius Pilate, "and of His own accord delivered Himself up to "death on the Cross, for us all."

In the Syriac Liturgy, called that of St. James the Apostle, which is the most common and most ancient of all the Liturgies, we read the following preparatory prayer for the sacrifice: "O God, who "in Thy mercy didst accept the sacrifices of the "ancient just, *accept also our sacrifice, and* "*favourably listen to our prayers.*" After the invocation, the deacon repeats the following prayer: "*Bless us again and again, by this holy* "*oblation, by this propitiatory sacrifice.*" Then, addressing the people, he says: "Bow down your "heads before the God of mercy, *before His pro-*

"*piliatory altar, before the Body and Blood of our Saviour.*"

In the Nestorian Chaldaic Liturgy, the Priest, at the offertory, says: "May Christ, who was immolated for our salvation, and who ordered us to commemorate His death and resurrection, *receive this sacrifice, presented by our unworthy hands.*" "May the Lord grant our requests; may He look favourably on *our sacrifice*, condescend to receive *our oblation*, and bless our *priesthood*. May the Holy Spirit of God repose on the offering of Thy servants; may He bless and sanctify it; and, since Thou hast called me to Thy pure and holy altar, to offer up to Thee *this holy and living sacrifice*, may He dispose me to receive this gift worthily."

In the Armenian Liturgy we read the following offertory of a Mass for the dead: "Holy Father, lover of men, receive *this sacrifice* in behalf of the departed; place their souls amongst the saints in Thy heavenly kingdom; may Thy divinity be appeased by *this sacrifice*, which we offer to Thee with faith, and may it grant rest to their souls." During the distribution of the Holy Communion, a canticle is sung, which, among other orthodox sentiments, contains the following: "This is the Body of Christ; this chalice is His Blood of the New Testament; Christ, the Word of God, is here present. He "is, at the same time, sitting at the right hand of His Eternal Father in heaven, *and offered up in sacrifice in the midst of us.*"

Most undoubtedly, these Liturgies, committed to writing at the commencement of the fifth century, contain the essential prayers, offered up at the altar, by the bishops and priests of the four preceding centuries of Christianity. The invariable agreement of all these different liturgies, their perfect uniformity in showing us throughout the Christian world, the oblation, the Victim, the unbloody sacrifice, the invocation asking the change of substance, the adoration and Divine Presence, could not have proceeded from the same cause, a cause equally imperative and obligatory upon all, namely, *that of divine institution.* Unless the apostles had expressly taught, both by word and by example, that those dogmas should be expressed in the celebration of the sacred mysteries, would they, could they have been found in all the liturgies of the Christian world, on their first appearance in writing?

The ancient liturgies, have now passed in review before us: we have everywhere beheld the altar, the oblation, the immolation of the victim, the unbloody sacrifice; we have listened to the invocation, asking the change of substance, which supposes, on the one hand, the real Presence, and on the other hand, adoration.

From north to south, from east to west, from the sandy scorching deserts of Africa to the frozen forests of Germany, from beyond the rivers Tigris and Euphrates to the Pillars of Hercules, (the Straits of Gibraltar,) we have heard identical words, expressive of the faith of the Sacrifice of the Mass, and of the real Presence, issuing from all sacerdotal lips, and, even with greater energy in the Oriental than in the Latin Churches. We have beheld all Christians approaching the altar with faith, with awe, and with adoration. Such was the universal belief, such the universal and daily practice of the Church in the golden ages of Christianity. The study of the Greek and Oriental Liturgies opened the eyes of the traveller Vansleb to the truth of the existence of the Sacrifice of the Mass, and of all the other Catholic doctrines rejected by Protestants, and determined him to embrace the Catholic faith. He died a Dominican friar.

Christ, therefore, at His last supper, on the eve of His Passion, *instituted a true and proper sacrifice*, as a continual memorial of His death; that His followers might have a sacrifice, at which they might assist in order to give *worthy* praise, adoration, and thanksgiving to God; to return to Him *acceptable* thanks; and daily to apply to their souls, the fruits of His Passion and death, as well for the remission of their sins, as for the obtaining of all good from Him, for both time and eternity. *This is the faith once delivered* by the *Apostles to the Saints;* (St. Jude, 3.) once put into the mouth of the Church; and which is not to depart from it, from henceforth and for ever; this is the faith preached by the apostles to all nations, and handed down to us by the divine rule of tradition, from generation to generation, without addition or diminution. But it is not enough, barely to believe the truth of this great mystery; our practice must coincide with our belief: we must respect its holiness, and endeavour to avail ourselves of the benefits which it is destined to confer on us. Let us then implore the Spirit of God, "without which, no one can understand the things that are of God," to set the truth of this sacrifice before our eyes in its proper light, make us believe it with an undoubted faith, and constantly influence our conduct towards it.

"Je ne sais quelle impression auront faite sur
"vous les extraits que vous venez de voir. Je
"vous avouerai franchement celle que j'en ai
"reçue. D'abord ils m'ont couvert de confusion
"à mes propres yeux; et avec ma condamnation,
"j'y ai trouvé celle du plus grand nombre de ce
"que nous sommes aujourd'hui de Catholiques.
"Quelle foi dans ces premiers Chrétiens, les uns
"si voisins de la révélation et de ses prodiges, les
"autres de ses témoins! quelle conviction de ses

" dogmes et de leur divine origine ! quelle énergie
" pour les exprimer ! quel concours, quelle piété
" et quel tremblement à la fois dans la participa-
" tion aux saints mystères ! quel zèle à s'en con-
" server dignes ! quel empressement à y retourner
" encore ! Il semble qu'ils n'habitent plus la
" terre ; ils y vivent commes des anges, méprisant
" tout ce qui flatte les sens : honneurs, richesses,
" plaisirs. Les douleurs, les tourmens, la mort
" même, rien de ce qui se passe, ne les touche ;
" l'éternité, le ciel, tel est le but qu'ils fixent : les
" bonnes œuvres, des mœurs pures, la prière et
" l'usage des sacremens, sont les moyens qu'ils
" prennent pour y arriver. Et nous, enfans dégén-
" érés d'une race si sainte, où en sommes-nous ?
" què faisons-nous ? Tièdes et lâches héritiers de
" leur nom, et de leur croyance, nous n'avons près-
" que plus rien de leurs vertus. Le monde, le plaisir
" et les affaires emportent le temps et les pensées
" de la plupârt. Incrédulité dans les uns, stu-
" pidité de foi dans les autres, indifférence prèsque
" en tous, jamais on ne vit plus de christianisme
" et moins de Chretiens. Voyez leur répugnance
" pour la table sacrée ; plusieurs l'abandonnent
" tout-a-fait ; plusieurs s'y traînent d'anneé en
" année par un reste d'habitude, et une sorte de
" décence : la tiédeur, l'irréflexion les y accom-
" pagne ; le dirai-je ? et de trop souvent même ceux
" qui montent à l'autel. Car les y aperçoit-on

" saisis de tremblement et de frayeur ? A la pré-
" cipitation des uns, à la froide accoutumance des
" autres, dirait-on qu'ils songent seulement au
" grand ministère qu'ils remplissent, à la victime
" divine qu'ils vont offrir pour le salut des peuples,
" au brasier ardent qui est entre leurs mains, et
" qui va passer à leur cœur, sans l'échaufer ?
" Peuples malheureux ! bien plus malheureux prê-
" tres ! d'où provient cette dégénération univer-
" selle ? J'en connois bien la racine ; et malgré
" les prétentions du siècle, je ne craindrai pas de
" la nommer : elle tient à notre profonde ignorance.
" Nous n'ambitionnons, nous n'apprecions des
" connoissances que sur les objets qui passent:
" nous sommes sans intérêt pour ce qui ne doit
" finir jamais. Nos jugemens, nos gouts, nos
" affections, notre vie entière n'est qu' une méprise
" complète, un funeste contre-sens, de la jeunesse
" au tombeau. *O curvæ in terras animæ et cœles-*
" *tium inanes !* Quelle sera donc la fin de ce
" désordre irréligieux ? Où nous mène ce renver-
" sement de la raison ? Je ne sais : mais il est
" impossible de ne pas se souvenir que l'extinction
" de la foi, suivant ce qui est écrit, doit un jour
" annoncer aux choses terrestres leur terme."
(Treverne, Bishop of Strasbourg in 1820.)

CHAPTER V.

ON THE FRUITS OF THE MASS.

"He that hath not spared even His own Son, how
"hath He not also with Him, given us all things?"—
Rom. viii. 32.

From what I have said above concerning the Mass, the reader will naturally suppose the fruits thereof to be very great. Nothing, indeed, can exceed the blessings which we might derive from it, if we made the best use of it. It is an oblation in which God delights, in consideration of which, He is prepared to grant us any graces. Let us descend to particulars.

The Council of Trent, in declaring, that "*by* "*means of the Mass, we obtain a share in the fruits* "*of the Sacrifice of the Cross,*" did but define against Protestants what had ever been believed, taught, and acted upon by all, everywhere throughout the Universal Church from the very dawn and origin of Christianity. The council in this decision, acted upon the rule, that we are not to admit any doctrine which has not been clearly handed down to us from the apostles, by an universal and uninterrupted tradition.

I will here confine myself to the testimonies of

two principal witnesses of the benefits to be derived from the Mass.

St. Chrysostom, A.D. 450, "declares that the "Sacrifice of the Mass is of the same efficacy as "that of the Cross." And St. Thomas Aquinas witnesses, that all the benefits which Christ gained to us by His Death, are to be found in the Mass. "Whatever," says he, "are the effects of the "Sacrifice of the Cross, are also the effects of the "Sacrifice of the Mass."

Our Saviour assures us that, whatever we ask the Father, in His name, will be granted to us. (St. John xvi.) How much more may we hope to obtain our wants when we offer Jesus Christ Himself, when His death, which is the fountain of all our good, is shown forth in such a manner as not only to be kept in our remembrance, but also to live in us, and to bring forth in us the fruits of life. There the blood of Christ most powerfully pleads for us; and not only the Passion and death of Christ, but also the victorious resurrection and triumphant ascension of our crucified King are here solemnly commemorated.

The fruits of our Saviour's passion and death upon the Cross, are thus applied to our souls by the Mass. Jesus Christ died upon the cross for all mankind in general; that is, He offered to God a full and ample satisfaction for the injury done Him by the sins of the world. In the Mass, by mystically renewing and presenting to His Father the death He suffered on the cross, He obtains His acceptance of the same, for the actual benefit of those in particular, for whom the Mass is offered up; by this means, those graces which He merited for mankind in general by His death, are actually applied to and bestowed upon our souls in such abundant manner, as our wants require.

The Old Testament was a figure of the New Testament, and the most remarkable events recorded in the former, are so many prophetic figures of what was to happen in the latter. Thus the deliverance of the Children of Israel out of the slavery of Egypt, was a figure of the redemption of man by Christ, from the bondage of Satan and sin; and the means ordered by the Almighty, for their deliverance, were a figure of what was to be afterwards done by our Redeemer for the deliverance of all mankind, from a far worse slavery; for as the Israelites were delivered from the Egyptian bondage by the offering up, in all their families, of the Sacrifice of an unspotted Lamb, and by sprinkling the door-posts of their houses with its blood, as a warning to the destroying angel not to injure anyone therein, and by the partaking of its flesh: so, we are delivered from the slavery of Satan and sin, by Jesus Christ, the true Lamb of God, being offered up as a sacrifice for us; by the sprinkling of whose blood, our souls are rescued from the power of Satan, and from the second death; of whose Sacred Flesh we are commanded to partake, in the Divine Mysteries, as an earnest of the share we have in Him, and in His sacrifice,—as a sovereign means of communicating to our souls the fruits of our redemption, and all the graces purchased for us by our Redeemer, as a pledge of our eternal happiness, and as a preparation and a viaticum for the great journey we are to make out of the Egypt of this world, to the true land of promise, to heaven the land of the living. Hence, St. Chrysostom says: "If the blood of "the figurative lamb protected the houses of the "Israelites, how much more will the Blood of the "true Lamb of God protect the souls of those "who are sprinkled therewith!"

As a Sacrifice the Mass is a standing memorial of our redemption; a daily communion with one another, by joining together in the solemn worship of sacrifice, as the children of God had always done from the beginning—a daily means of uniting ourselves in those mysteries with Jesus Christ our high priest and victim, and of coming to God with Him and through Him.

It is also the victim and sacrifice of the New Testament, by means of which we are enabled to give worthy praise and homage to God; to return Him acceptable thanks, to obtain the remission of all our sins, and all good both for time and eternity.

Those four great and indispensable duties, correspond with the same number of God's most prominent perfections under which He appears to us. For He is our Sovereign, our Benefactor, our Judge, and the Source of all our good. Inasmuch as He is the Supreme Ruler of Heaven and earth, we are obliged to acknowledge His supreme and inalienable dominion over us, and our total and essential dependence on Him: which duty we perform by *adoration:*—inasmuch as He is our Benefactor, we are bound to manifest our deep sense and gratitude for the numberless blessings, favours, mercies, benefits and graces which we are continually receiving from Him: this duty we perform by *thanksgiving;*—inasmuch as He is our Judge, it behoves us to appease His wrath which we are continually incurring by our sins: this we do by *satisfaction;*—and inasmuch as He is the Source of all our good, it is to Him alone that we should have recourse in all our necessities, spiritual and temporal: and this we do by *impetration.*

Under the Mosaic dispensation, there were four kinds of sacrifices, corresponding with the four great duties which we owe to God, viz., holocausts, sin-offerings, thank-offerings, and peace-offerings; whereas, in the New Law, the Sacrifice of the Mass answers all the ends and purposes of those four kinds of sacrifice, and in an infinitely superior manner; nay, in a manner worthy of God.

Thus, by means of the Mass, we are enabled to offer up to God the highest adoration, the most acceptable thanksgiving, the most powerful propitiation for our sins, and the most effectual impetration for obtaining all our wants, spiritual and temporal.

1st. As to *Adoration:* as rational creatures, made by God, and for God, we owe to Him our homages of adoration, praise, and glory, as to our Maker, our first beginning and last end, our Supreme Good, our chief felicity, and perfect happiness. To Him do we owe all the love and affections of our hearts and souls; we are indispensably obliged to dedicate and consecrate ourselves for ever to His service.

But how little is all that we can offer to Him of our own!—how little is all we can do of ourselves, when compared with the homage, adoration, praise and thanksgiving, due to the infinite majesty of God! If the whole creation could be made a holocaust or burnt-offering for the glory of God, it would be no more in His eyes, than if a grain of chaff were to be burnt in honour of some earthly monarch; for the whole creation compared to God, is less than a grain of chaff compared to an earthly monarch, or even to the whole creation. How greatly then are we indebted to the Son of God, who, by the institution of the Sacrifice of the Mass, has furnished us with a means of rendering to God the full homage due to Him, an homage worthy of Him; the Mass being a sacrifice of infinite value, by reason of the infinite dignity of Him who is both Priest and Victim therein.

All the honour that the angels and saints in heaven have ever given to God, or will ever give Him by their adorations and praises—all the honour that men upon earth have ever given, or will give to God, by their acts of religion, their good works, their penances, and even by suffering martyrdom to testify their fidelity to Him, will never approach, nor bear comparison with the honour that God receives from one offering up of the Sacrifice of the Mass. For all the honour that can be rendered by creatures to God, is but a limited honour; whereas, God receives in the holy Sacrifice of the Mass an unbounded, unlimited, and infinite honour, in every respect worthy of Him.

The eternal Son of God made man, there and then humbles Himself in the most profound manner, by assuming the forms of bread and wine, and by offering Himself up by the hands of the Priest, under the appearance of death, on purpose by the humiliation of His humanity, which receives infinite value from its union with the

Divinity, to render to His Eternal Father for us, and with us, the most perfect homage. When therefore we join our intention with that of our High Priest and Victim, Jesus Christ, and offer this holy sacrifice to God in acknowledgment of His sovereign dominion over us, and in protestation of our total subjection to Him, we do Him sovereign honour; we give Him perfect honour and glory, the greatest that is possible for a creature to give to his Creator. It is then that we give Him the honour due to His name, it is then that we can say to God with David: "According "to Thy name, O Lord, so also is Thy praise." (Psalm xlvii.)

2nd. By the Sacrifice of the Mass, we are enabled to render to God *acceptable, equivalent*, and *worthy thanks*. One of the principal duties which God requires of us, is to have a just value of the favours, bounties, and mercies He bestows on us, and a grateful sense of our obligations to Him. Hence the Holy Ghost says, by the mouth of the royal Prophet: "The sacrifice of praise "shall honour Me; and this is the way by which "I shall show them My salvation." (Psalm xlix.) Christ Himself said to the Samaritan, whom He had just cured of the leprosy, and who came and prostrated himself before Him, giving Him thanks, "Were there not ten made clean, and where are "the nine? There is no one found to return and

" give glory to God but this stranger." " Go thy way," said He, " for thy faith has made thee whole." (St. Luke xvii. 16.)

And St. Paul says: (1 Thess. v. 18,) "In all "things give thanks to God in Christ Jesus, " for this is His will concerning you all." Moreover, he that expects a continuance of God's favours and benefits, must, as a means to obtain them, return thanks for those already received. But what do we not owe to God for our creation and redemption, for our preservation and vocation, and for so many other benefits, especially that eternal free love of His for us, which is the source of all these benefits?

How little is all that our store can afford towards discharging this immense debt! how good then has God been to us in furnishing us, by means of the Eucharistic Sacrifice, with a standing fund to enable us to discharge this infinite debt, and to render to Him a full and adequate thanksgiving, worthy of Him! In order to enable us to defray this debt, the Son of God Himself became man to make Himself our Priest and Victim; and in that quality, to offer up in our behalf a worthy sacrifice of thanksgiving, no less infinite, by reason of the dignity of His person, than those favours and mercies for which He makes this return of thanks for us: this sacrifice of thanksgiving He once offered upon the Cross, and offers daily in the Eucharist, upon a million of altars throughout the world; in which offering, He expects that His whole family of heaven and earth should join with Him, that with Him and through Him, they may make a daily return of worthy thanks for all God's blessings bestowed upon both Him and them.

3rd. The Sacrifice of the Body and Blood of Christ, is also a *sin-offering, a sacrifice of propitiation for obtaining mercy and pardon for our sins.* It was principally to remit and destroy sin, that this sacrifice was instituted.

For this purpose was this sacrifice offered on the Cross; for the same purpose is it still continued to be offered on our altars. "This (said "Christ Himself) is My Blood of the New Testa-"ment which shall be shed for many *for the "remission of sins.*"

The debt contracted to the divine justice by sin was infinite; nothing that any mere man, or even all mankind put together, could do or suffer, for the expiation thereof, would bear any kind of proportion with it, or go any part of the way towards the canceling of it. Therefore did the Son of God assume a body, in order to become our victim. (Psalm xxxix.) This Body He offered in sacrifice upon the Cross for the sins of all mankind; with this, He paid our ransom, and completely redeemed us: this same

Body He has bequeathed to us in the Sacrament and Sacrifice of the Blessed Eucharist, in which as our Priest and Victim, He daily appears before His Father in our behalf, and presents His Passion and Death to Him to obtain the forgiveness of our sins. The Sacrifice of the Eucharist is therefore truly *propitiatory*, in virtue of the Blood of the New Testament, the fruit of which it applies to our souls.

Accordingly, the Council of Trent declares, that "the Almighty, being appeased by the oblation of "the Holy Sacrifice, imparts the gift of repentance, "and forgives all sins and crimes however great." (Sess. xxii. 6.)

What an advantage it is to our souls, to have daily celebrated amongst us, this *propitiatory* sacrifice, in which the Lamb that taketh away the sins of the world, presents to His Eternal Father upon our altars, under the mystical veils that represent His Death, His Body as broken and slain for us, and His Blood as shed for our sins;—and in which, with His Body and Blood, He intercedes to obtain mercy and pardon for us! What sinner can despair of the forgiveness of his sins, (if, like the prodigal child, he desires to return home to his true Father,) when he sees here before him, as it were, bleeding upon the altar, the Victim, by whose blood all our sins were cancelled;— when he sees the great High Priest of God and man, offering a sacrifice for the remission of his sins?—"Let us therefore, go with confidence, to "this throne of grace, that we may obtain mercy, "and find grace in seasonable aid." (Heb. iv. 16.)

We stand in great need of this sacrifice of propitiation; we owe a great debt to the Divine justice for our numberless sins. Let us recount to ourselves, in the bitterness of our souls, all our years past. Did we not very early break through our baptismal engagements, profane God's temple within us, affront the Spirit of God, and tread under our feet the Blood of the Son of God? Have not our sins been multiplied from that time till now? "What shall we offer to the Lord that is "worthy of Him? Wherewith, shall we kneel "before the high God?" (Mich. vi. 6.) *Neither holocausts, nor thousands of rams, nor yet our own blood, can expiate our guilt. The Blood of Christ alone would do it;* with this, we kneel before the Most High, when we assist at the Sacrifice of the Altar, where this blood is applied to our souls. Nor is this blood applicable to our own souls only: the inexhaustible treasures of mercy, which are laid open in those sacred mysteries, give us a confidence to join all here in a body, with our great Advocate and High Priest at our head, and to plead for mercy through this same blood for our brethren, both living and dead, that we may obtain for them all, the remission of their sins, and the discharge of all the debts and punishments due to them.

The Sacrifice of the Mass does not actually remit sin, like the Sacrament of Penance. It only renders the Almighty propitious to sinners, by presenting to Him His only-begotten Son, who offered Himself up a Victim on the altar of the Cross for their salvation; and who, by continuing this same Sacrifice, is continually making intercession in their behalf: the Almighty, being thus propitiated, becomes merciful to them, and grants them the virtues of contrition and compunction. He also inspires them with a horror of their sins, opens their eyes to the fatal consequences thereof, and inspires them with resolutions of amendment of life. Being thus, through the Sacrifice of the Mass, prepared and disposed for the forgiveness of their sins, they have recourse to the Sacrament of Penance, in which they receive the full remission of their sins, and final reconciliation with God.

Fourthly, and lastly,—The Sacrifice of the Mass is an *impetratory* sacrifice. The Eucharist is offered up, not only for the adoration and praise of the Almighty, in thanksgiving for all His benefits, and for the remission of our sins; but also for obtaining all graces and blessings from God, through the Blood of Jesus Christ. "No "one can come to the Father but by Him." (St.

John xiv. 6.) But here in the Mass we approach God by Him, and with Him, as to our High Priest and Victim. Christ says, (St. John xvi. 23.) "*If you ask the Father anything in My name "He will give it you.*" How much more salutary is this sacrifice of supplication, in which we not only ask in the Name of Jesus Christ, but come with His Sacred Blood, before the throne of grace, where He Himself pleads (in Person) for us!

Christ is continually at the right hand of His Eternal Father, pleading for us : "who is at the "right hand of God, making intercession for us." (Rom. viii. 34.) This, He particularly does during the offering up of the Holy Sacrifice. Our creed represents Him as sitting on the right hand of God in heaven. During the Mass, He, as it were, stands up, and shows His Eternal Father His wounds, which He has received for our sakes ; upon which the Father, calling to mind the perfect obedience of His only-begotten Son, is affected, and beams upon us a look of mercy and of compassion.

If Christ, by means of His Passion and Death, is the only source of all mercy, grace, and salvation to man; when and where can the fruits and effects of His Passion be more certainly and more abundantly bestowed upon us, than while assisting at the Holy Sacrifice of His Body and Blood, where the whole mystery of His Passion and

Death is renewed and commemorated, and which He ordained for the very purpose of bestowing on us the blessed fruits of His Passion and Death?

If we knew that all the angels and saints in heaven were praying for us, with what confidence, with what hopes, should we not be inspired, of obtaining all manner of graces! But it is certain that one prayer of Christ is more powerful and efficacious, for obtaining all kinds of graces for us, than the prayers of all the saints together. "His prayers are always granted, on account of "the respect due to His Divine Person, and of the "right He has acquired by the merits of His Pas-"sion and Death;" and it is particularly during the Mass "that He offers up prayers and supplica-"tions with a strong cry and tears to Him who is "able to save us." This is the fountain of salvation, from which all ought to draw the waters of grace: it is hence that the good man must derive vigilance under temptation, fidelity to divine grace, and power and strength to fulfil the commandments.

The sinner should come and draw hence, in sorrow of heart, the detestation of his sins, and amendment of life. In all our necessities, whether spiritual or temporal, let us therefore fly to the altar, that we may obtain seasonable aid and help, and that we may obtain strength to overcome our passions, to correct our evil inclinations, and adorn our souls with every virtue.

Many and great are our necessities, both general and particular; and great are the miseries to which we are liable. Of ourselves, we can do nothing: we can neither believe, hope, love, nor repent, nor even make a step towards our justification and salvation without the help of heaven. We are, moreover, encompassed on all sides with dreadful dangers, that threaten us with the worst of evils, for both time and eternity. But, in the Sacrifice of the Mass, Christ has furnished us with an inexhaustible fund, out of the fountains of our Saviour, to supply all our necessities, to heal all our infirmities, to guard us against all dangers, and to redress all our miseries. Let us, therefore, run to Christ, our High Priest, and our Victim, and *with Him*, and *through Him*, to His Eternal Father, and He will give us all good, together with Himself, the Supreme Good.

In this sacrifice of supplication, we are not limited or confined in our addresses, as if we were to ask and receive graces for ourselves alone; for, as we have here the Victim slain for the general redemption of the whole world, and as the High Priest, the God-man, here appears before His Heavenly Father on behalf of all mankind, we are authorized to put up our petitions with Him, and through Him, for the general necessities of the whole Church of God and of all mankind :—that the Holy Name of God may be sanctified by all, that His kingdom of grace may be propagated through all nations and through all hearts; that His will may be done by all, and in all things; that the Church may be exalted by the sanctity of her prelates and pastors; that all infidels, heretics, and sinners may be converted; that all errors and abuses may be corrected; that we may be preserved from war, plagues, famines, and other evils; and that, being delivered from the hands of our enemies, we may serve God without fear, in holiness and justice before Him all our days.

All these, together with many other graces and blessings, we are encouraged to ask in this Sacrifice, where Christ is both our Priest and Victim: accordingly, the priest, in offering up the chalice, says, "We offer to Thee, O Lord, this chalice of "salvation, imploring Thy clemency, for our own "salvation, and for that of the whole world."

Lastly, the inexhaustible treasures of mercy, which are laid open in these mysteries, give us a confidence to join, all in a body, and to plead for mercy, through this same Blood, *for our departed brethren*, that we may obtain for them a discharge of all the debt of punishment due to their sins. If it is a holy and salutary thought to pray for the departed, that they may be delivered from their sins, how much more efficacious will our prayers be when joined with the adorable Sacrifice of

Christ's blessed Body and Blood, and offered up to God in union with those divine mysteries!

Accordingly, the Council of Trent declares, "that there is a purgatory, that the souls of the "departed there detained, are helped by the "prayers of the living faithful, and especially by "the most acceptable Sacrifice of the Altar; and "that the practice of offering up this Sacrifice, "not only for the living, but also for the dead, is "derived from the teaching of the apostles." (Sess. xxii.)

"DES INTENTIONS DANS LESQUELLES ON DOIT DIRE "OU ENTENDRE LA SAINTE MESSE.

"Adorons les intentions toutes divines, dans "lesquelles Notre-Seigneur s'est offert en sacrifice "sur la Croix, et s'offre encore tous les jours, par "le ministère des Prêtres sur nos Autels. Il veut "rendre à Dieu les grands devoirs d'adoration, de "remercîment, de satisfaction et de prière; et "pour le faire en la manière la plus parfaite, son "amour le porte à s'immoler-soi-même, et à se "faire notre Prêtre et victime tout ensemble.

"O qu'il nous y apprend bien, comment, et à "quelle fin, il faut entendre ou dire la sainte "Messe! Quelles louanges, quels remercîmens, "quels hommages, ne lui devons-nous pas rendre "pour une telle conduite!

"Avec quelles intentions donc assistons-nous
"à la Sainte Messe? Est-ce pour adorer la
"Majesté de Dieu et toutes ses divines perfections,
"qui ne peuvent être dignement adorées, que par
"cette sainte et précieuse Victime, qui est immo-
"lée sur nos Autels?

"Est-ce pour reconnaître sa bonté envers nous,
"et lui rendre grâce pour tous les biens qu'il nous
"a faits, et qu'il fait encore tous les jours avec
"profusion à toutes les créatures, dont nous ne
"saurions le remercier comme il faut que par
"cette divine Hostie?

"Est-ce pour appaiser sa Justice, et pour
"réparer l'injure que lui ont faite nos péchés dont
"la grandeur demande une satisfaction infinie, et
"pour lesquels il n'y a que Jésus qui puisse
"pleinement satisfaire?

"Est-ce pour demander quelques grâces pour
"nous ou pour les autres, n'y en ayant point de si
"grandes, qu'on ne puisse obtenir par Jésus, qui
"s'offre particulièrement à Dieu son Père dans ce
"Sacrifice pour tous les besoins de son Eglise?

"Mon Dieu, puisque les Prêtres qui disent la
"sainte Messe, et ceux qui l'entendent, vous
"offrent le même sacrifice que votre Fils vous a
"offert sur l'arbre de la Croix, il est bien juste
"que les uns et les autres entrent dans ses inten-
"tions, et qu'ils se proposent la même fin que lui.
"Faites-nous en la grâce, ô mon Dieu! et ne

"permettez pas que nous en ayons aucune, qui
"ne convienne à la sainteté de l'Hostie qui vous
"y est offerte, à laquelle l'Eglise nous avertit
"de nous rendre conformes."—(Tronson, Sulpiien mort en 1676.)

In a word, "La Messe est le grand sacrifice,
"l'oblation unique, la resource du genre humain,
"promis à l'univers depuis le commencement des
"siècles. C'est la seule Victime que Dieu regarde
"d'un œil favorable, la seule capable de désarmer
"sa colère, lorsque les péchés des peuples l'ont
"irrité. Le Prêtre est le sacrificateur de la nou-
"velle alliance. Il parait à l'autel, à la place
"de Jesus Christ, formant son Eglise par sa
"mort, s'immolant de nouveau pour elle, et
"l'affermissant contre tous les efforts de l'enfer."
—(Massillon.)

"*The Holy Mass gives to God the greatest
"honour that can be given to Him; nothing so
"much weakens the power of Satan; it imparts
"the greatest relief to the souls in purgatory; it is
"the most powerful means of appeasing the wrath
"of God against sinners; and it imparts to man-
"kind the greatest spiritual advantages during
"this life.*"—(St. Liguori.)

"*While the Mass is being offered up, the Holy
"Trinity is honoured and praised; the angels
"are rejoiced; the Church is edified, and receives
"help and grace; sinners obtain repentance and*

"*pardon; the souls in purgatory obtain refresh-*
"*ment and rest; and those who offer up the*
"*Sacrifice, together with those who worthily assist*
"*thereat, obtain a powerful remedy against their*
"*daily sins and infirmities.*"—(à Kempis.)

The Mass, as a sacrament, is to the faithful an inexhaustible source of grace; it has this advantage over all the other sacraments, that it imparts to the soul the very Source itself from which all graces flow, by giving us Jesus Christ Himself, the author of all graces, His Body, His Blood, His Soul, and His Divinity; and, therefore, it is the most excellent of all the sacraments, in itself, and in its fruits. Accordingly, Christ Himself says: "This is the Bread
" which came down from Heaven; I am the
" Living Bread which came down from heaven.
" If any man eat of this Bread, he shall not die;
" if any man eat of this Bread, he shall live for
" ever." (St. John vi. 50.) "Amen, amen, I say
" unto you, except you eat of the Flesh of the
" Son of Man, and drink His Blood, you shall not
" have life in you. He that eateth My Flesh and
" drinketh My Blood hath everlasting life, and I
" will raise him up in the last day. For My
" Flesh is meat indeed, and My Blood is drink
" indeed. He that eateth My Flesh, and drinketh
" My Blood abideth in Me and I in him. As the
" Living Father has sent Me, and as I live by the

"Father, so he that eateth Me, the same shall "live by Me." (St. John vi. 52.)

Our Saviour elsewhere, (St. Matt. xxii.) compares the participation or communion of the Holy Eucharist to a banquet to which a certain rich man had invited all his dependants, but many of whom, making excuses, declined his invitation. Upon which, the master, being angry, said: "Those men that were invited, but did not come, "shall not taste of my supper."

The Church, alluding to the Eucharist, sings: "O sacred banquet, in which Christ is received, "the memory of His Passion kept up, the soul "filled with grace, and a pledge given of the glory "to come!"

Again, the Eucharist, as a sacrament, is the Living Bread, the food, the nourishment, the strength, and the life of our souls, the manna of heaven, the tree of life, spirit, truth, and life itself. It is the remedy of all our evils, the most powerful medicine for all our diseases, the sovereign antidote against the poison of the infernal serpent, the comfort of our banishment, the support of our pilgrimage, the price of our ransom, the earnest of our eternal salvation.

As sin and death, and all our woes, originally came to us by eating of the forbidden fruit; so grace and life, and all our good, come to us by eating of the fruit of this Tree of Life. The very institution of those heavenly mysteries, to be the support of our spiritual life for the time of our mortality, implies a command for us to approach them, and to make use of them. We should be guilty of self-murder, if we suffered our bodies to perish by refusing to take that food which God has appointed for their sustenance; and are we not equally guilty of murdering our souls if we suffer them to starve for want of the food and sustenance which our Lord has allotted them in this life-giving banquet? Truth itself assures us that without this heavenly food *we have no life in us*. As, then, we are most strictly bound to maintain the life of our souls, we are most strictly bound to use this food of life; and it is no less certain death to stay away from this Blessed Sacrament, than to come to it unworthily.

Here, we receive an assurance of the share we have in our Redeemer, and in the Sacrifice of His Cross. Here, we are mystically incorporated in Him, and are made partakers of His Spirit. Here, we are admitted to that Blood which is the seal of the new covenant, importing the remission of our sins, and our reconciliation with God, through the death of His Son, together with admittance to all graces and blessings through Him. Here, not only the Passion and Death of Christ, but also the victorious Resurrection and triumphant Ascension of our crucified King, are solemnly commemorated. Here we have a most certain pledge of a happy resurrection, of everlasting life, and of eternal enjoyment in the happy country of Him who thus gives Himself to us in this place of banishment. Here, finally, He gives Himself to be our food, our comfort, and support in this pilgrimage, till, by virtue of that food He brings us to our true country, where He will give Himself to us for all eternity.

Let us then bring to this Sacrament a lively faith and a serious consideration of the work we are about; let us consider who it is whom we are about to receive; how great and glorious, how pure and holy it is. Also let us conceive a most profound humility and awful reverence for these tremendous mysteries sanctified by the real presence of Jesus Christ Himself, the Lord of glory and the fountain of all sanctity. Let us then annihilate ourselves in the sight of this great Lord and maker of heaven and earth. Let us fear and tremble in consideration of our manifold treasons against Him, and our base unworthiness. For it is the Holy of Holies who lies here concealed under those sacramental veils!

CHAPTER VI.

THE EXCELLENCE OF THE SACRIFICE OF THE MASS.

"This is My beloved Son, in whom I am well pleased."
—St. Matt. xvii. 5.

What the sun is to the material world, the Mass is to religion. As it is the sun that gives light, warmth, and fertility to the earth, so it is the Sacrifice of the Mass that is the life and soul of religion. As, without the sun all would be darkness in the world, and everything on the face of the earth perish, so without the Mass the same effect would be produced in religion. The Mass is the keystone of the arch of the edifice of Christianity, which holds together all its parts. The Mosaic sacrifices gave way before this adorable Sacrifice, as the imperfect light of the moon and stars vanishes before the blaze of the sun. The Mass is the centre of the system of the Christian religion, around which all its other parts, as so many planets, move, and by which they are influenced. Every other part of religion has some reference and tendency towards it, or derives from it its meaning.

This great Sacrifice commenced with the world,

was consummated on the Cross, and is continued on our altars. When we assist thereat, we are engaged in the most sacred, the most august, the most sublime action that can possibly be performed by man on the face of the earth. We render to the great God that made us, the most supreme worship, the most divine homage, adoration, and thanksgiving, that can be possibly offered to Him by His creatures. Earth has nothing equal to it; heaven nothing greater. It is the Palladium of the world, and an inexhaustible source of all blessings, to both the living and the dead.

It is a magnificent reality which, while it perpetuates the great sacrifice of Calvary, accomplishes all the figurative sacrifices of the Mosaic Law, and renders to God all the glory and satisfaction due to Him. It is the principal fountain of our Saviour, from which all ought to draw the waters of grace. Though omnipotent, God has nothing greater to bestow on us; though full of wisdom, He cannot give us anything more valuable; though most rich, He has no greater treasure to bestow upon us, than that which He has given us in the Sacrifice of the Altar. It is because we cannot, by any other means, offer to God an equal degree of worship, because we cannot offer Him anything else with which He is equally pleased, or upon which He has promised to look down with equal favour and complacency, that the Church *commands* all her children to assist at this redoubtable sacrifice on all Sundays and other particular days.

"La Messe est, de toutes les actions du Chris-
"tianisme, la plus glorieuse à Dieu, et la plus
"utile au salut de l'homme. Jésus-Christ y
"renouvelle le grand mystère de la Rédemption;
"il s'y fait encore, dans un vrai Sacrifice quoique
"non sanglant, notre victime; il vient en per-
"sonne, nous appliquer, à chacun, les mérites de
"ce sang adorable qu'il a répandu pour nous tous
"sur la Croix.

"Les saints Prêtres ne regardoient l'autel,
"qu'en tremblant; ils n'y montoient qu'avec une
"sainte horreur: plus leur vie étoit sainte, plus
"ils étaient attentifs à conserver leur ames pures,
"plus ils se trouvoient souillés en la présence de
"l'Agneau sans tâche qu'ils alloient immoler."—
(Massillon.)

The excellence and dignity of a sacrifice is estimated by the excellence and dignity of the victim that is offered, of the priest that makes the offering, and of the ends for which the offering is made. Now, all these things concur to recommend, in the highest degree, the sacrifice of the Blessed Eucharist, which in substance is the same as that which the Son of God offered once upon the cross; because, the Victim is the same, the Chief Priest the same, and both the one and the other answer the same ends, though in a different manner. Let us then admire the excellence of this great Sacrifice, which is offered on our altars; a sacrifice in which the whole passion and death of Jesus Christ is solemnly acted by Himself in person, and in such a manner, that He Himself is both the Priest and the Victim, the Sacrificer and the Sacrifice! Christ Jesus, the Son of God, was the great high priest of God and men, who once solemnly offered His own Body and Blood upon the Cross, a sacrifice to God for all mankind; His Body and Blood were the Victim by which we were redeemed. And now this same great High Priest of God and men officiates in Person in the Sacrifice of the Altar, and there offers up the same Victim of His Body and Blood to His Heavenly Father in our behalf. Can anything be more divine than such a Sacrifice, in which a God is the Priest, and a God the Victim!

As often, then, as we go to celebrate or assist at these sacred mysteries, we should represent to ourselves, that we are called upon, as by a royal proclamation from heaven, to be sanctified, and to come, together with our great High Priest, Jesus Christ, the Son of God, and with His whole Church of heaven and earth, to join in a most solemn sacrifice, that is going to be offered to God, for all the great ends above mentioned.

It is a most certain truth, that in this divine sacrifice, we present ourselves at the altar of God, before the throne of His mercy, with Jesus Christ His Son at our head, in the society of His whole family, the whole people of God, wherever they are; for the sacrifice is offered by Jesus Christ in the name of them all, and with the concurrence of His whole Church. We here offer up to God the most acceptable victim that can be presented to His divine Majesty; the most agreeable adoration and thanksgiving that can be offered to Him; the most powerful atonement for sin, and the most effectual means for obtaining all graces and blessings, it being the offering up of the Passion and Death of the Son of God.

It has always been inculcated by the ancient Holy Fathers, that the Church, in all her religious worship, has nothing to present to us, that can, in any degree, be compared with the wonderful presence of Jesus Christ, in the Eucharistic sacrifice. Every office has some relation to it; almost every ceremony is a distant preparation towards worthily celebrating it, or receiving it; it is the principal object, towards which all the thoughts and desires of a true Christian here below, are directed; it is the reward of his labours, the comfort of his exile, the nourishment of his piety, his support during his pilgrimage, his strength in dangers and afflictions, his only hope when he descends into the grave, because, the surest pledge of a glorious resurrection, and of a happy immortality. It contains the history of the greatest benefit ever conferred on man, that upon which all his hopes are founded, by representing our divine Redeemer, dying for the salvation of the world.

The bloody immolation was made on the cross; the oblation is renewed on our altars, and will continue till the end of time, the only Sacrifice of the New Law, which has superseded every other sacrifice, and can alone henceforward, be acceptable to the Supreme Being.

When Moses, with whom God was wont to converse familiarly, beheld clouds of smoke issuing from the summit of Mount Sinai, as from a fiery furnace, and lightning continually flashing; when he heard the sound of a trumpet becoming continually louder and louder; when he beheld all the other preventive measures which God had ordered, in order to make His sanctity respected, he was seized with fear and awe, and exclaimed: "*I am fright-*"*ened and tremble*." But what was all this that terrified the mediator of the old law, when compared with what takes place on our altars? It was no more than a mere shadow. The Christian Priest and the faithful, who constitute with him but one ministry, are here come to the "city of the living "God, to the heavenly Jerusalem, to the com-"pany of many thousands of angels; they are "associated with the Church of the first-born, "whose names are written in heaven, with God "the Judge of all, with the spirits of the just "made perfect, and with Jesus, the Mediator of "the New Testament; the sprinkling of whose "blood speaketh better things than that of Abel." (Heb. xii. 22.)

When, in the old law, the High Priest, on the yearly festival of expiation, was about to enter the Holy of Holies, to pray for himself and for the whole people of Israel, what preparatory prayers, fasting and sacrifices were then offered up by the command of God Himself! The precious vestments which he wore were significant of the excellence and holiness of the function which he was then about to perform. While the people remained without, fervently praying in solemn expectation, he entered with his hands full of the blood of the victim into the Holy of Holies. He remained there but a few moments, praying with fear and awe; the ark of the covenant being enveloped in a cloud of the smoke of incense. But what is all this in comparison with what takes place on our Christian altars? Jesus, the Angel of Great Counsel, our great High Priest, passes thence into the highest heavens, and presents our Victim on the high altar above. He enters into the perfect tabernacle, not made with hands. He carries with Him, not the blood of goats or of calves, but His own precious blood, in order to obtain eternal redemption. If, then, the ministration of death was glorious, how much more is the ministration of the Spirit in glory! If the ministration of condemnation was glorious, how much more does the ministration of justice abound in glory! (2 Cor. iii. 9.) That which in the old law appeared glorious, was not glorified by reason of the glory that excelleth. If the Mosaic sacrifices, which have been done away with, were glorious, how much more glorious is the Sacrifice of the Mass, which is to remain for ever!

It is God's delight to be with the children of men. Hence the Holy of Holies continually blazed with a light which proceeded, not from the sun, nor from any natural source, but from a divine brightness issuing from the Mercy-seat; yet this light was but the shadow of God's presence. The fulness of His divine presence, we must never forget, He has reserved for us, among whom He is now present, not in shadow, but in the truth and substance of His own Divine Person, in the Holy Eucharist. We can never sufficiently admire the perfection and the height of glory to which God has raised His Church, which stands midway between the synagogue and the heavenly Jerusalem, and is but one step removed from the glory of heaven. The synagogue had but the *shadow* of the divine presence: the Christian Church has, in the Eucharist, the *reality* thereof, but *veiled;* whilst the angels and saints in heaven have the reality of the divine presence *unveiled.* We are but one remove from the glory of heaven.

It is to the eyes of faith alone that the greatness and the holiness of the Mass appears; for in it we adore a hidden God, we immolate an invisible Victim, we offer up an unbloody sacrifice.

The Mass is a sacrifice, offered up at all times, and in all places, which has ever continued since the origin of Christianity, and shall be perpetuated till the consummation of ages.

I. *It has been ever offered up since the origin of Christianity.*—From that moment in which Jesus Christ delivered to His apostles, and to their lawful successors, that consoling precept, "*Do this in* "*remembrance of Me,*" the Mass has been continually offered up. Until churches were built the apostles continued to "*break bread from* "*house to house.*" (Acts ii. 46.)

It has been offered up at all times.—The varied revolutions of the great luminary that enlightens our system, would seem to have no other object nor end, but continually to perpetuate this august oblation; for when it ceases to be offered up in one part of the globe, other priests, in other lands, succeed them in this awful function.

It is a *perpetual sacrifice*, a mystery which the Church will incessantly renew and perpetuate, until she herself is consummated in eternity.

It will always endure "*the same*" till the end of ages. *The Church is always uniform as to the essentials of the sacrifice;* she can never suffer them to be altered; she is always careful to preserve in their original purity the dogmas of the mystery, that the faithful may safely join in an oblation, which has the glory of God for its essential end, and the salvation of their immortal souls for its great object.

It is the *morning sacrifice*, in which is offered up the Lamb slain from the commencement of the world; the *evening sacrifice*, which will be offered up till the consummation of ages.

II. The Mass is a sacrifice which is offered up *in every place*, from the rising of the sun to the going down thereof. Wherever the Church of Christ exists, and it exists everywhere, ministers consecrated by the same unction, inheritors of the same powers, invested with the same character, address to the Almighty the same supplications, offer up the same Victim, pour forth the same Blood.

III. The Mass is an *holocaust* to honour God; a *thank-offering* to express our gratitude for benefits received; a *sin-offering* to counteract the effects of the divine indignation; a *propitiation for sin;* a sacrifice of *impetration* and *prayer* to obtain all necessary graces; lastly, an *act of consecration* to attach to the worship of God everything which, by its nature, is devoted to His service. It is, in a word, a sacrifice which supplies the place of every other oblation, supersedes every other sacrifice, disannuls every strange offering, and in some manner absorbs every degree of merit, homage, and adoration, due to the Supreme Being.

IV. It is a sacrifice in which not only the members of the Church militant on earth participate, but also the citizens of heaven, by the union of their homages, and the sorrowful inhabitants of the place of expiation, by the resources which they thence derive for their deliverance from their fiery probation.

V. It is a sacrifice *destined to efface all our sins.* Jesus Christ is in the Mass, the Lamb of the Passover, by whose virtue we pass from death to life; from the captivity of sin to the liberty of the children of God; from this land of exile to our true home in the abodes of eternity. We no longer stand in need of the blood of heifers nor of an emissary goat; we no longer ground our justifications on bloody aspersions; we no longer are obliged to seek a separate victim to efface each particular stain; we possess in the *one Victim* which is immolated on our altars, a superabundance of merits, which extends to all the maladies of our souls.

It is a sacrifice offered up for all our *necessities*: they are all embraced by and included in the merits of the oblation which Jesus Christ makes of Himself, and are expressed in the prayers that accompany it.

Lastly, the Mass is a sacrifice in which *everything is holy*, whether we consider the supreme object of the offering, the Victim which is offered, or the Priest by whom the offering is made. It is to the incomprehensible majesty of the Eternal Father that the offering is made; it is Jesus Christ that is offered to His Eternal Father; and it is in the name and in the person of Jesus Christ that the sacrifice is offered.

Every day, does the blood of the Lamb flow from our altars to the place of expiation of the souls in purgatory. Every instant, some happy soul, purified by this expiatory effusion, wings its flight to the realms of everlasting repose.

Lastly, this holy sacrifice is full of mysteries and of miracles; the Eucharist itself is a profound mystery; the sacrifice is another; and the priesthood a third. The more the miracles are multiplied, the more *there are of wonders and mysteries*.

The institution of the eucharistic sacrifice and

sacrament is one of the three great proofs of God's love to mankind. His love for us brought Him down from His heavenly throne to become one of us ; His love for us made Him offer Himself up upon the altar of the cross a sacrifice for our sins ; and His love for us made Him bequeath to us His Flesh and Blood, that we might partake of the merits of His incarnation and redemption.

The eucharistic sacrifice and sacrament is one of the three great means by which Christ communicates Himself to us. He took upon Him our flesh, to make us partakers of His divinity, and to carry us up to heaven. He offered Himself up as a sacrifice for us, to deliver us from sin and hell, and to purchase for us mercy, grace, and salvation ; and He gives us verily and indeed His flesh and blood, to be the support of our pilgrimage, till, by its virtue, He brings us to our true country, where He will feed us for all eternity.

Thus, in His incarnation and birth He made Himself our companion; in His Passion and Death, the Victim of our ransom ; in the banquet of His last supper, our food and nourishment; and in His heavenly kingdom, our eternal reward.

The Son of God became one of us that He might become our High Priest and Victim. He offered Himself as a sacrifice for us all, that He might open the gates of heaven to us. His sacred Body and Blood are here offered up for us, and received by us, in remembrance of His passion and death, and as a pledge of eternal happiness.

In a word, these three great mysteries are, as it were, so many links of the same chain; the mystery of the Eucharist is indispensably necessary to communicate to our souls the benefits of the mysteries of His Incarnation, Passion and Death. Without the mystery of the Eucharist, the benefits of the mysteries of the Incarnation and Death of Christ would be, to some extent, lost to us. Christ's design in redeeming us, would have remained in a manner incomplete.

It is through Christ alone that we can have access to God; and it is principally in the Mass that we have this access. It is by Christ, the Priest and the Victim of the Sacrifice of the Mass— with Christ—and in Christ, that all honour and glory are given to God the Father, in the unity of the Holy Ghost.

It is by, or *through Christ alone,* who is the Victim of the Sacrifice of the Mass, that we are enabled to render to God the *full* homage that is due to Him. Our hands being defiled with sin, the Almighty could receive from us no homage worthy of His supreme majesty. Without Christ, how could we presume to draw nigh to the Godhead, whose eyes are too pure to behold our evils, and who cannot therefore look upon our iniquities? (Habacuc i. 13.) For this reason, was Christ given to us, that the vileness and corruption of our nature might no longer be an obstacle to the homage due by us to the Godhead; but that, being purified by our union with Him, we might honour Him as He deserves to be honoured. Thus, *through Christ*, we are enabled to render to the Deity every kind of honour, to fulfil every kind of homage, and to make to Him every kind of atonement. Wherefore, there should be no longer any bounds to our feelings of gratitude. The *immensity* of God is honoured, since it is the universal sacrifice of all places that is offered. The *eternity* of God is honoured, since it is the sacrifice of all times that is offered; a sacrifice that shall have its consummation in eternity only. The *sanctity* of God is honoured, since it is the High Priest of spotless purity who offers by our hands. His *justice* is acknowledged, since it is the great Victim of Propitiation that is immolated. His mercy is seconded, since it is the mediator between God and man, the angel of peace, that wafts the grateful odour of the holocaust, even to the altar on high. Behold what we are capable of doing through the Sacrifice of the Mass! Behold the various degrees of honour that we are enabled to render to the Almighty through it! Although, owing to the corruption of our nature, we are unworthy to approach the Divine Majesty, yet, by means of the Mass, we are enabled to render to God all honour and glory.

It is with Christ that we offer.—The ministry which the priest exercises is not a mere image, a bare representation of the Sacrifice of the Cross; *but a positive renewal of the first immolation.* The action which he performs is identified with that performed by Christ Himself. When the priest blesses the oblation, it is Christ that imparts to the offering the value that sanctifies it. When the priest raises his eyes towards heaven, or extends his hands in prayer, Christ presents to His Eternal Father, His own hands, pierced with wounds, and purpled with His own Blood. When the priest renders thanks, when he humbles himself, or bewails his own offences and those of the people, Christ also renders thanks and implores the clemency of His Father. He reminds Him of that contrition, of that grief for sin, which once rent with mortal anguish His bosom in Gethsemane. In a word, the priest does nothing without Christ; he becomes, in some measure, another Christ; a visible Man-God to the people. A visible representation takes place here on earth of what is performed by the sovereign High Priest on the high altar of heaven. The association of both the priest, and of every one of the faithful, with Christ, in offering up the holy sacrifice, imposes on them a strict obligation of being holy, even as Christ Himself is holy.

Lastly, *it is in Jesus Christ* that this sacrifice is offered; in Him alone, is all the merit and all the value of this sacrifice contained. It is upon Him alone, that God beams a look of mercy; and it is by this benign look of mercy being reflected upon us, that we are sanctified and saved. Hence, we are not to place our confidence in any of the exterior ceremonies that accompany the sacrifice; nor in the recital of the prayers employed in offering it up: in order to fulfil the ends of the sacrifice we must be united to Christ. In Him shall we find all that sanctity of which we are so deficient, and that degree of attention and fervour which our weakness is unable to attain. In Him, all our thoughts become holy, our desires pure, our will upright, and under perfect restraint. In Him, we become strong, notwithstanding our frailty; steadfast, notwithstanding our inconstancy; and just, notwithstanding the corruption of our nature. In Him, we render honour and glory to the Eternal Father; we acknowledge Him to be the principle of all things; we avow our total and essential dependence upon Him; we confess His power, anticipate His justice, solicit His mercy, and bless Him in all His works.

The Mass, considered as a *prayer*, is the most

affecting, and most devout compilation ever made by man. In what other place shall we find collected, in so small a compass, such vehement acts of sorrow, such profound acts of humiliation, such lively sentiments of gratitude, such expressive acts of thanksgiving, such fervent prayers of supplication, such admirable tributes of adoration, to the great Creator of heaven and earth? Where else shall we find such beautiful allusions to all the great mysteries of religion; such powerful means of strengthening our faith, animating our hopes, and filling our breasts with the love of God? Here we are presented with an abridgment of our whole religion, and an epitome of all its mysteries; here we behold, at a single glance, all the obligations that the Gospel imposes on us; here, in some measure, we obtain a glimpse of all the promises which faith makes to us, together with a foretaste of that happiness which is destined for us by the mercy of God. Thus, the Christian who is instructed in the sense and spirit of the Mass, and of its ceremonies, finds all that can enlighten his mind and nourish his heart.

"Adorons Notre-Seigneur Jesus-Christ, se pré-
"parant à offrir sur le Calvaire *son sacrifice qui*
"*est le même que celui que nous offrons tous les*
"*jours sur nos Autels.*

"Regardons cette action comme une action

" toute divine, et qui, étant la plus importante
" que nous puissions faire, demande aussi une plus
" grande préparation !

" Faisons paraître par la retenue de nos sens,
" par la posture de notre corps, et par tout notre
" extérieur, une humilité profonde, une crainte
" religieuse et une vive foi de la présence de Dieu.

" Disons la sainte Messe, avec un air de modes-
" tie et de dévotion qui fasse connaître à ceux qui
" l'entendent, combien nous sommes convaincus,
" et combien ils le doivent être, que Jésus Christ
" y est réellement présent, accompagné d'une
" multitude d'anges qui l'adorent.

" Faisons attention à la dignité du souverain
" Prêtre, au nom et en la personne duquel nous
" agissons ; à la sainteté infinie de la Victime,
" qui s'immole entre nos mains ; et à la majesté
" incompréhensible de Dieu, à qui nous offrons ce
" sacrifice.

" Sic vivam ut *sacrificium illud adorandum,*
" *tremendum ac Deo plenum* quotidiè merear
" offerre."—(Tronson.)

PRAYER.

I confess, O my God, that of myself I cannot possibly assist at these divine mysteries as I ought. I can neither think a good thought, nor speak a good word, nor offer up a prayer which may be acceptable in Thy sight, except Thy grace direct me, and Thy Holy Spirit assist me. Grant me, therefore, Thy poor supplicant, to feel, sometimes at least, some little of the cordial affection of Thy love, that my faith may be strengthened, my hope in Thy goodness increased, and that my charity being once perfectly enkindled, by having tasted the Manna of Heaven, may never decay. Amen.

CHAPTER VII.

ON THE CEREMONIES, LANGUAGE, VESTMENTS, INCENSE, LIGHTS, ETC., USED IN THE LITURGY OF THE MASS.

Interior religious worship comprises sentiments of faith, respect, gratitude, confidence, love, and submission to God. Exterior religious worship, or ceremonies, is the expression of those sentiments.

The word *rites* means those religious ceremonies which are approved and enjoined by the Catholic Church.

The word *liturgy* means the collection of prayers and ceremonies by which the august sacrifice of the Mass, the most excellent act of religion, is performed. Ceremonies, or exterior worship, are necessary to nourish and manifest interior worship, the worship of the heart, by which we acknowledge God and His supreme dominion over us.

Before entering on a particular explanation of the ceremonies, language, vestments, &c., of the Mass, I may in general observe that the meaning of them would never be enquired, if people would reflect that the Mass is not like the forms of worship which we behold around us, of modern date and domestic origin; otherwise, like them, it would betray by its language and the paucity of its ceremonies, the land and the time of its birth. The Mass is the worship of the Christians of old; it is therefore redolent of antiquity: it reminds us at each step of the habits and manners of nations which have long ceased to exist. We therefore revere and cherish it as the form after which our forefathers in the faith worshiped, when they first embraced our holy faith, and which they had received from those who had derived it from the apostles of Christ. A worship fabricated of late years may be anything else, but it cannot be the worship of the Primitive Church.

ON CEREMONIES.

"Let all things be done decently, and according to "order." (1 Cor. xiv. 40.)

God Himself in the old law, and the Church in the new law, has ordained many sublime ceremonies, capable of inspiring us with reverence and awe for the sacred mysteries of religion. Religious ceremonies are outward signs of the interior dispositions with which we ought to be animated while worshiping the Almighty; they are also means of exciting those dispositions in us. Let us then look upon them with the eyes of faith; let us behold and practise them, with the greatest sentiments of humility and reverence; let us never forget that they are but helps to acquire true internal dispositions of religion; let us then endeavour to acquire the interior virtues of the soul, by outward acts of religion, and thus render ourselves pleasing to our Creator.

Ceremonies are also a kind of illustration of our sacred mysteries; they, to a certain extent, represent them to the eye, as a book or a discourse does to the ear or mind, especially to the uneducated, who are always the greater number. Every one who has ever assisted at the solemn celebration of divine service at any considerable Catholic establishment, or in any cathedral abroad, must have felt how much the splendour and magnificence of Catholic worship must tend to excite the spirit of devotion, and inspire the soul with respect and awe.

ON THE LANGUAGE OF THE LITURGY.

The languages generally approved of by the Church in her public liturgies, are the Greek in the Eastern Church, and the Latin in the Western Church, of which we form a part; these having been the two prevalent languages at the time of the establishment of Christianity. In the course of ages, the original Greek and Latin languages ceased to be the vernacular; for the modern Greek language differs nearly as much from the ancient Greek, as the modern Italian does from the ancient Latin. Nevertheless, the Catholic Church has ever continued the use of the two original languages in her public worship; in which respect, she has done no more than did the Jewish Sanhedrim in similar circumstances; for after that the Jews had, during the Babylonish captivity, exchanged their own original Hebrew for the Syro-Chaldaic tongue, they continued to perform divine service in the Temple and in the synagogues in their primitive Hebrew language, although the common people no longer understood it. Nor did our Saviour, who, with the apostles, regularly frequented public worship in the temple and in the synagogues, ever blame them for so doing. Likewise both the United and Schismatic Greeks still retain, in their public divine worship, the use of the original Greek language, as the Western Church does the Latin, although it is no longer understood by the common people, who speak different modern dialects.

Not only does the Church approve of the above practice, but also forbids her ministers to use in the Mass the vernacular tongue of the nation to which they belong.

As the doctrine of the Church, like her Divine Founder, is "yesterday, and to-day, and the same for ever," she has wisely ordained that the ancient Greek and Latin, which, being now dead languages, never vary, be alone used in the liturgy, to avoid the dangers of a variable language, which is the character of every modern tongue. Great would be the danger to the faith, besides many other inconveniences, of using public worship in a language which is always changing or growing obsolete. Of all languages, the Latin is the only language universally understood.

Moreover, Catholics look upon their priests as the ministers of Christ. Hence, when they stand at the altar, they become mediators between God and His people. They have a sacrifice to offer, which is an act that passes between God and them alone; to complete which, no assistance of the people is necessary. They offer for the people, but, in the strict sense of the word, the people have no part in offering with them. It is then no matter of consequence in which language the Almighty is addressed. He who is the author of all languages equally understands them all. If the priest understands the language in which he then addresses the Almighty, what more is requisite? The words by which sacrifice is offered are addressed to God, and not to the people, nor by the people; and if he who addresses them, and He to whom they are addressed understand them, every useful object is attained, and nothing more is required.

Lastly, a universal language, not liable to change, is indispensable as a bond of union in a universal Church, to maintain a correspondence between its different parts, and to keep the different national Churches attached to the centre of Catholic unity. Intelligent and unprejudiced Protestants readily admit this.

As diplomacy has its particular language, which formerly was the Latin, and is now the French language, in which nations correspond with each other; and as a congress could not be held unless all the representatives of the different nations thoroughly understood and could fluently express themselves in one particular language, so the general affairs of the Catholic Church could not be transacted, nor General Councils of the Church held, unless all the bishops of Christendom understood and spoke one and the same language. Therefore, the dignity and the safety of the Church required that the Greek language, in which the Christian religion had been taught in the East, should continue to be the ecclesiastical language there, and the Latin language, in which the Christian religion had been taught in the West, should likewise continue to be the ecclesiastical language of the Western Church.

So far is the Catholic Church from wishing to

keep the people in ignorance, by retaining her original and apostolical languages, the Greek and Latin, that she strictly commands her ministers to inculcate the Word of God and the lessons of salvation to the people, in their vernacular tongue, on every Sunday and festival of obligation throughout the year, and frequently to explain to them and make them understand the nature and meaning of her divine worship. Moreover, the Ordinary of the Mass is to be found in most Catholic prayer books, together with a translation into the different European languages.

Lastly, in all Catholic prayer books, under the title of *Devotions for the Mass*, are found prayers corresponding with every part of the Liturgy, and most proper to excite the sentiments and acts of devotion which the faithful ought then to feel. Thus, while the priest remains at the foot of the altar, they are taught to make acts of contrition and of general confession of their sins; at the Creed, to make acts of faith in the principal Christian mysteries; at the Offertory, to offer up the bread and wine for the great ends of sacrifice; during the Canon, to make to God supplications for all persons and for all their wants; at the Elevation, to adore with the priest; and at the Communion, to partake of the Sacred Mysteries with him. The only difference is, that those sentiments and desires are expressed in language better adapted to common understandings, and consequently more useful to the generality of people.

ON THE USE OF PARTICULAR VESTMENTS OR ROBES DURING THE MASS.

In all the public functions of his office, the priest wears certain appointed robes, or vestments, especially when he offers up the Holy Sacrifice. God Himself in the old law, condescended to regulate what robes the Priests and Levites should wear while performing their respective functions: the Church in the new law, has done the same for her ministers. The robes in which bishops and priests appear at the altar, were the ordinary apparel at the time of the commencement of Christianity. The bishops and priests had particular suits of robes of the ordinary fashion, but of a superior quality, which they wore at the altar only. If then, at the present day, the robes of bishops and priests differ from common apparel, it is because the Church continues, in her public worship, to make use of the kind of robes that were in common use at the time of her institution, whilst the fashions of nations have since then undergone numberless changes. In appearing in particular robes while performing their sacred functions, the ministers of religion do no more than what judges and magistrates do in the performance of the functions of their respective offices. By invariably preserving the ceremonies, language, and robes, in use at the time of her institution, the Catholic Church furnishes us with a strong presumption of the Divine origin and apostolicity of her doctrines; for if the Church has been so particular and careful in preserving things of less moment, as ceremonies, language, &c., how much more careful must she have been, in preserving in their pure and unadulterated state the doctrines taught by Christ and His apostles, which are matters of much greater importance.

ON THE USE OF INCENSE.

The use of incense is borrowed from the practice of almost every nation in religious worship. Pagans burned perfumes in the presence of their idols. In the Levitical law, there was, by the command of God Himself, an altar of incense, as well as a perpetual fire, that burned continually before the ark of the covenant. St. John, in the Apocalypse, represents the angels of heaven, as occupied in offering up incense in golden censers before the throne of the Eternal; which incense, he tells us, is the prayers of the saints. It is a most beautiful and expressive ceremony. The circling clouds of smoke, which ascend to the vaulted roofs of the temple, are an admirable representation of the aspirations which should ascend from our hearts to heaven. The sweet odour of the perfume most expressively teaches us, how agreeable to God is fervent prayer. These allusions are certainly beautiful, and should teach us henceforward to repeat with great feeling those words of the Psalmist, "May my prayer, O Lord, "ascend like incense in Thy sight." For these reasons, the Church uses incense in many of her offices; but in none more than during the solemn sacrifice. Twice during Mass, does the priest offer this perfume; first, at his going up to the altar; and again after the Offertory. The server continues to offer incense during the Elevation. We offer this incense as a mark of honour to any creature towards which we have religious respect, as well as to God Himself. In this, it differs from sacrifice, which can be offered to the Deity only. We incense the altar, out of respect for it, because it is soon to contain the precious Victim; we incense the bread and wine, on account of their being destined to become our Victim. The incense, before being used, is blessed by the priest, with the sign of the cross, accompanied with these words, "Mayest thou be blessed by Him, in whose "honour thou art going to be burnt." And, during the incensing, he prays as follows: "May "this incense, which Thou hast blessed, ascend "to Thee, O Lord, and may Thy mercy descend "upon us." Thus, you observe that nothing can be more edifying than the prayers and sentiments with which the Church accompanies the ceremonies of her solemn service. If every Christian would but enter into the spirit of them, he would find in them that help to devotion which they are intended to convey.

ON THE USE OF HOLY WATER.

"They shall dip hyssop into the waters, and sprinkle "therewith all that are defiled: in this manner they "shall purify the unclean."—(Numbers xix 10.)

The waters here mentioned were the waters of purification or lustration, which in the old law, were blessed by mixing them with the ashes of the red heifer, that had been offered up in sacrifice, and entirely burnt, as the expression of their faith and hope in the future sacrifice of Christ. These ashes contained and imparted to the waters the virtue of purifying from all uncleanness those who received them with proper dispositions. This ceremony is striking and impressive, and has, for this reason, been adopted by the Church. Hence, the ministers of the Church, previously to divine service, sprinkle the faithful with holy water, using those words of David which have an evident reference to the waters of lustration: "Thou "shalt sprinkle me with hyssop and I shall be "cleansed: Thou shalt wash me and I shall be "whiter than snow." (Psalm l.) This is done to remind the faithful of that interior purity with which they ought to enter the house of God, and to induce them to pray the more earnestly for that disposition.

The water is first blessed by the minister of the Church, as is everything else which is used in the service of God. "Every creature of God," says St. Paul, (1 Tim. iv. 4, 5.) "is sanctified by prayer." The blessing consists in offering up prayers that every person or place, where it shall be sprinkled, may be guarded from pestilence and other calamities, and secured against the assaults of wicked spirits.

The water is next mixed with a little salt, which is an emblem of wisdom and of incorruption, over which, a prayer has been read by the priest; the blessing is then completed. The faithful use it with piety, hoping that the prayers of the Church, joined with their own prayers, may obtain this blessing for them from the Almighty.

This practice is useful, and conformable to the purest principles of religion.

ON ALTARS.

Sacrifice and altars are correlative terms: the one supposes the other. As sacrifice dates from the creation of the world, so do altars. It was God Himself that showed to Adam how to build an altar, and to offer sacrifices thereon. The Israelites had their altars, especially those of holocausts and of incense. "The Christians "also," (Hebrews xiii.) "have altars, whereof "they have no power to eat who serve the Taber- "nacle." As, then, Christians have altars, so they must have a sacrifice.

A crucifix is always placed on the altar, over the tabernacle, to remind the faithful that the sacrifice of the Mass is a continuation, a representation, and commemoration of the sacrifice of the cross, and to warn them that it is to God alone that this supreme act of religion is referred, and not to the saints or martyrs.

ON THE TAPERS WHICH ARE LIT UP DURING THE MASS.

This is a remnant of primitive Christianity. In times of persecution, the first Christians performed divine service in catacombs or dwellings underground, and in secret and hidden places; also before daylight. Pliny, the Younger, being Proconsul in Asia Minor, informed the Emperor Trajan that the Christians were wont to meet before daylight, to celebrate their mysteries, to sing hymns to their Christ, to encourage each other not to commit any crime, but to lead a virtuous life.

The use of lights was then indispensable.

The Church continues to use them on her altars during divine service, as an emblem of Christ, who is "*the light of the world, the light that enlightens every one that enters the world;*" (St. John i.) as a symbol of the faith of Christians in the real presence of Christ on our altars in the Blessed Eucharist, and as the expression of their faith in general, of which lights are a symbol. "Thy word, O God," says David, "is a lamp to my feet, and a light to my steps." (Ps. cxviii.)

Within the sanctuary, and in front of the altar, a lamp is kept lit day and night, to warn us that

Jesus Christ, the light of the world, is present on our altars, awaiting our adorations and homages, in order to confer on us His graces; and that our lives should, by their holiness, shine like a luminary. Moreover, we must bear in mind that perpetual adoration is due to our Divine Saviour in the holy Sacrifice and Sacrament of the Eucharist; but, as we are incapable of this, we substitute in its place inanimate creatures, particularly a flame, which is an excellent emblem of devotion.

If, in the old law, a perpetual fire was, by the command of God, kept continually burning before the Holy of Holies, which was illuminated by the shadow of God's presence only, how much more ought we, in the new law, to keep a continual light burning before our tabernacles, where the reality of Christ's presence personally resides! It is a matter of great regret that so many Catholics leave to the lamp the whole of the duty of worshiping Christ in our tabernacles.

If a person were going to the court of an earthly monarch, on his way thither he would think of where he was going, and compose himself accordingly; in like manner, when a person is about to enter a church to assist at the holy sacrifice, or to adore our Saviour in our tabernacles, he should recollect the greatness of Him whom he is about to visit, and that it is into the presence of the King of Kings that he is about to enter. This thought should inspire him with respect and awe, for, when on entering the church, he beholds the lamp burning, it should warn him that the Lord of Glory there resides, and that he should immediately fall down and adore.

" Do this in commemoration of me." — *St. Matthew* xxvi.

" The fruits of the Sacrifice of the Cross are imparted to our souls by the Sacrifice of the Mass."—*C. Nice*, Sess. 22.

SECOND PART.

EXPLANATION OF THE LITURGY OF THE MASS.

CHAPTER I.

ON THE INTENTIONS AND DISPOSITIONS WITH WHICH WE SHOULD ASSIST AT THE MASS.

"The daily renewal on our altars in the Mass, of the "Passion and Death of Christ, by which heaven and "earth were reconciled, being the most holy and the "most divine act of religion, the Council of Trent strictly "enjoins every care to be taken, and every diligence to be "used, that all, both priest and people, should bring to it "the utmost purity of conscience, piety of heart, and "outward marks of respect and devotion." (Sess. xxii. Decretum de observatione.)

"By faith, Abel offered unto God a sacrifice exceeding "that of Cain." (Heb. xi.)

"With desire," said Christ, (St. Luke xxii. 15,) "have "I desired to eat this Pasch with you before I suffer."

It was our Saviour's most anxious desire to celebrate with his disciples the first Mass. It is still His most ardent wish to celebrate it now with us, because every time this sacred action is performed, we renew the memory of His sacred Passion, we offer Him supreme worship, we promote His greatest glory, and the joy of the heavenly spirits; we advance our own sanctification, and loose the chains of captive souls. St. Augustine declares that, though omnipotent, God can give us nothing greater; though full of wisdom, He can think of nothing more valuable; though most rich, He has no greater treasure to bestow on us, than what He has given us in the Sacrifice of the Mass. How thoughtless, then, and ungrateful, would it be on our part, to set no value on this treasure, and to neglect availing ourselves of it!

The first of murderers did not fail to offer the sacrifice pointed out by the natural law. He presented what was marked out as the matter of the holocaust. To have seen him engaged in this religious exercise, who would not have regarded him as a faithful adorer? But all the value and merit of his sacrifice were rendered ineffectual, because his heart was not right before God, and because, unlike his brother Abel, he walked not in innocence and simplicity.

David says to God: "If Thou hadst desired "sacrifice, I would indeed have given it; with "burnt offerings Thou wilt not be delighted. A "sacrifice to God is an afflicted spirit: a contrite "and humble heart, Thou, O God, wilt not "despise." (Psalm l. 18.) We here see that no outward means of honouring God and appeasing

His wrath, even by sacrifices appointed by Himself for that purpose, will find acceptance with Him, unless accompanied with sincere intentions of mind, and dispositions of heart.

ON THE INTENTIONS AND DISPOSITIONS WITH WHICH WE OUGHT TO ASSIST AT MASS IN ORDER TO REAP THE FRUITS THEREOF.

Those intentions and dispositions are as follow: —1. A most profound humility, awful dread and respectful reverence for the great God whom we there adore, founded on the incomprehensible Majesty and supreme dominion of God over us and over all creatures; on the infinite sanctity of Jesus Christ, who is present on our altars in those sacred mysteries, as our High Priest and Victim.

2. A deep sense of the numberless blessings, favours, mercies, benefits, and graces, which we have been continually receiving from our good God, from the first moment of our existence to the present, accompanied with a heart full of gratitude, for so much goodness, so liberally bestowed on us, who have been so undeserving of it.

3. A humble and sincere repentance for all our sins, accompanied with an ardent desire, and firm resolution of never, for the time to come, offending our good God.

4. A steady and unshaken confidence in the

goodness of God, that through the merits of His Beloved Son, offered up to Him in this holy Sacrifice, He will pardon our past sins, enable us to persevere in His service for the time to come, bestow on us every good thing, of which He knows we stand in need, and bring us at last to eternal happiness.

5. As the Mass is not a mere simple figure or remembrance of the Passion and Death of our Saviour, but a mystical representation, an actual commemoration and continuation of the same, according to that saying of St. Paul, "as often as "you shall eat this bread and drink this chalice, "you shall show forth the death of the Lord until "He come," (1 Cor. xi. 26.) we should endeavour to put our souls in the like dispositions of repentance for our sins with which, as good Christians, we, should have assisted at the Sacrifice of the Cross, had we been present thereat.

6. We should assist at the Mass with *confidence;* for nothing should more inspire us with this disposition than the presence on our altars of Jesus Christ offering Himself as our Victim of propitiation and of impetration to His Eternal Father.

7. *With respect;* for Jesus Christ offers Himself to God there for us, and we offer ourselves to Him by the hands of the Priest. These considerations should induce us to assist at the holy

Sacrifice with the utmost respect of which we are capable.

Those persons are particularly wanting in respect towards our holy mysteries, who, by their wilful distractions and outward irreverences show that they are not actuated by any religious sentiments and feelings. Those also are wanting in like respect, who, being in the state of mortal sin, assist at the Mass without any desire, or even thought of repentance for their sins; for such, by assisting at Mass, become guilty of the greatest hypocrisy, inasmuch as they pretend to honour God and implore His mercy and protection, while in reality they insult and irritate Him.

If then, it is provoking God for wilful and obdurate sinners to assist at Mass, why does the Church oblige them to assist thereat? The Church does not oblige sinners to assist at Mass in a state of impenitence and obduracy; but warns them at least to desire to repent, and to assist at the holy sacrifice with sentiments of faith, humility, and compunction; for the Church forbids the holy sacrifice to be offered up if those who are to assist thereat are not likely to manifest by their deportment proper intentions and dispositions. But though a person may not be actually penitent, providing that he desires and asks of God the gift of repentance, and courage and strength to begin a new life, he may with advantage assist at the holy Sacrifice, for such a desire of reconciliation with God is a gift of the Holy Ghost, and in order to derive any benefit from the Mass, sinners must have at least this commencement of repentance.

Enable us, therefore, O God, by Thy grace, "so to commemorate the Passion and Death of "Christ Thy Son, as to partake most plentifully "of the fruits of it."

CHAPTER II.

EXPLANATION OF THE COMPONENT PARTS OF THE LITURGY OF THE MASS.

"When the priest stretched forth his hands and "offered up the blood of the grape, all the people fell "down upon their faces, to adore the Lord their God, "and to pray to the Almighty God."—Ecclus. l. 16-19.

The Liturgy of the Mass may be divided into four parts: the preparation of the people; the preparation of the matter of the sacrifice; the canon; and the communion. The two first *essential* parts of the *sacrifice* of the Mass are contained in the canon or third part of the liturgy of the Mass. And the *communion* or third essential part of the sacrifice is contained in the fourth part of the liturgy, which also bears the name of communion; and contains the prayers which precede and follow this last part of the sacrifice.

FIRST ARTICLE.

PREPARATION OF THE PEOPLE.

The preparation of the people is subdivided into two parts, the penitential and instructive parts.

The Penitential Subdivision.

"A sacrifice to God is a humbled spirit. A contrite "and humble heart, Thou, O God, wilt not despise."— Psalm l.

Robed in his sacerdotal garments, the priest, intrusted with the most august and most redoubtable ministry, proceeds with humility and awe to the foot of the altar, where he is to consummate the great act that reconciles heaven and earth.

Of all the dispositions with which we should approach the altar of God, humility and contrition of heart are the most essential. Woe to that man who encompasses the altar of God and is present at the august sacrifice, without feeling a regret for his sins, and a desire to be freed from them! And who is altogether free from sin? "If," says St. John, (I. Ep., i.) "we say that we have no sin, "we deceive ourselves, and the truth is not in "us." St. James says, (iii. 2,) "in many things "do we all offend."

Wherefore, the priest commences the Mass at the foot of the altar: he does not presume to ascend to it till he has first humbled himself before God, and implored His mercy and forgiveness. Like the publican, he stands afar off, striking his breast, and acknowledging his unworthiness.

Those sentiments of humility and contrition which should animate both priest and people while at the foot of the altar, are contained in the following prayer.

"Enter not into judgment with Thy servants,
"O great God, for in Thy sight no man living
"shall be justified; but look on the face of Thy
"Son Jesus Christ, who in the Garden of Geth-
"semane, was pleased to take upon Him all my
"sins and to suffer a most dreadful sorrow, a
"bitter agony and bloody sweat, in order to cancel
"the bond that stood against me, and to cleanse
"my soul from all its pollutions. I this day
"desire to join the humble contrition of my soul
"with the agony of Jesus in the Garden, and in
"union with this most holy Sacrifice of His Body
"and Blood. Look upon me, O my God, with
"the same almighty eye of mercy with which
"Thou wast pleased to pierce the heart of Peter
"after his unhappy fall, and as I have but too

"often, by my repeated infidelities to Thee, imi-
"tated his fall, so grant that I may now rise
"after his example by a perfect conversion, and
"like him persevere to the end in serving Thee
"and promoting Thy glory."

The priest commences by making on himself the sign of the cross, together with an express invocation of the Most Holy Trinity; because it is in the name and in honour of the Holy Trinity that he is about to renew the sacrifice of Christ's Passion and Death.

He then recites, alternately with the ministers, the forty-second Psalm, which is one of preparation to the sacrifice, and which was used as such during the Mosaic dispensation.

This Psalm encourages him, notwithstanding his unworthiness, not to be dejected, but to put his confidence in God, and to approach His altar with a cheerful heart; because the Almighty, who is our salvation, will make glad the hearts of all who confess to Him, and put their trust in Him. He implores the assistance of the Almighty against his enemies; he reproves his soul for being disheartened, while it ought to trust in God; and finally, he prays to God to illuminate and console him. The priest recites this psalm alternately with the ministers of the people, because the people, as well as the priest, should excite themselves to approach the altar with faith and confidence, in order to offer up the sacrifice by the hands of the priest. The psalm closes with the doxology. It was Pope St. Damasus that, in the fourth century, introduced the custom of repeating it after every psalm. The former part of it is of apostolical origin; the latter was added by the General Council of Nice, to express the eternity, and consequently the Divinity of the Three Divine Persons.

THE CONFITEOR.

"The just is the first accuser of himself."—Proverbs xviii.

"Confess your sins to one another," says St. James, "and pray for one another, that you may be saved."—v. 16.

While at the foot of the altar, the priest, though encouraging himself not to be dejected, but to put his confidence in God, does not lose sight of his unworthiness. He therefore makes, together with the people, a general and public confession of his sins.

In the old law, previously to the offering up of sacrifice, a general confession of his sins was required from the High Priest. An acknowledgment of sins is still more necessary in the new law, as a preparation for the sacrifice.

The formulary of confession of sins, used by the Church, consists of two parts: in the former, we confess to the Almighty, and to the whole court of heaven, that we have sinned exceedingly in every way, in thought, word, and deed; and in the latter part, we appeal to the whole court of heaven, to pray to the Almighty, to obtain of Him for us the remission of our sins. This confession is mutually made, by both priest and people; they repeat the prayer, which contains an avowal of the sins of which they are guilty. It is first made by the priest, because he should set the example of those holy dispositions, and testify and acknowledge that he stands in need of the same indulgence which he solicits for others. Conscious of his unworthiness, and of the holiness of the function which he is about to perform, he calls on God for His assistance, saying: "Our "help is in the name of the Lord, who made "heaven and earth."

He commences thus: "*I confess to Almighty* "*God :*"—that is, I accuse myself, in the presence of Almighty God, of all the injustices of my past life. Not only does he confess to God, and to "the spirits of the just made perfect, who, at "the last day shall sit in judgment on us," but also to his fellow creatures on earth. The angels and saints have been witnesses of his sins; he therefore acknowledges his guilt in their presence, that he may conciliate their intercession. First, he makes this confession to the purest and most merciful of Virgins, who herself never knew the least defilement of sin; to an archangel, who triumphed over the chief of the rebellious spirits and over his followers; to the Baptist, the most holy of men, who was the friend of the Spouse; to the two chief apostles, SS. Peter and Paul, the most powerful of all the saints upon earth, who were invested with the power of binding and unbinding consciences; and lastly, *to all the saints*, the friends of God, and to his own brethren *on earth*. What does he confess? Why does he call to witness, God, His angels, and His saints, heaven and earth? He calls them to witness his acknowledgment of having been most unfaithful and treacherous to his God.

Has he not, at least, respected some of the faculties of his soul, and of the senses of his body? No! he has defiled them all; for he has sinned, in thought, in word, and in deed! Everything in him has been made an instrument of sin. Could any prayer be better calculated to inspire a spirit of repentance, which is the soul of penance? Striking his breast, in imitation of the publican, who by his humility found mercy before God, he says: *through my fault,* for I have had so many motives, and means of avoiding sin; *through my fault,* my perversity has alone been the cause of my sins; I do not attribute them to either the occasions of sin, or to the violence of temptation; *through my most grievous fault,* my sins are most grievous, owing to the obligations of my baptism, and to the great and numerous graces that, in preference to many others, I have received from God.

The second part of the *Confiteor* consists of an invocation of all the angels and saints to pray to God for him.

Sinking under the burden of his sins, he says, Shall I despair? God forbid! religion inspires me with other sentiments; it commands me to pray, and to invoke all the angels and saints, that they may pray to God in my behalf; *therefore,* that is, *because* I have been guilty of so many grievous sins, *I beseech the Blessed Virgin, &c.* I no longer presume to address God directly; I confine myself to entreating all the saints of heaven, and my brethren on earth, who have been witnesses of my sins, to become my intercessors with my Lord and my God.

By means of this general confession of sins, made by both priest and people, a sort of concert, a kind of unison of sighs and tears is established. How different is it from what is heard in heaven! There the blessed spirits bow down in adoration before the dazzling glory of Omnipotence, and cry out, "Holy, holy, holy, Lord God of armies!" Here a crowd of sinners fall prostrate before the tribunal of their Judge, and cry aloud for mercy: "*I have sinned, through my fault,* "*through my fault, through my most grievous fault.*"

The two absolving prayers, *Misereatur* and *Induljentiam*, which immediately follow the *Confiteor*, and which mean, "May the Lord have "mercy on us, forgive us our sins, and bring us "to life everlasting;" and "May He grant us "pardon, absolution, and remission of all our "sins," these prayers, I say, are not authoritative, but supplicatory prayers, being used in the same sense by both priest and people; for in them the priest makes himself a part of the people.

With the following short and energetic expressions, do the priest and his ministers terminate the prayers which detain them at the foot of the altar: "O Lord, cast a look of compassion on "us; then shalt Thou enliven our hearts, and "Thy people will rejoice in Thee. Show us, O "Lord, Thy mercy, and grant us Thy salvation. "O Lord, hear my prayer, and let my cry come "unto Thee."

Thus the devotion with which the faithful ought to be occupied while the Priest remains at the foot of the altar, is chiefly to excite themselves to sorrow for their sins, which render them unworthy to be present at the sacrifice, and earnestly to beseech the Almighty to remove the cause of their unworthiness. They should then particularly implore the grace of God, which alone can discover to them the malice of sin, and obtain for them true repentance.

The last words which the priest pronounces at the foot of the altar, are *Dominus vobiscum;* by which he prays that Christ may be in the midst of them, that the Spirit of God may repose on them, that He would grant them the spirit of prayer, and the dispositions of fervour and repentance, so necessary to obtain the object of their supplications.

The priest then ascends to the altar and kisses it.—The language he holds while ascending, is perfectly conformable to the dispositions which the preceding preparatory prayers are calculated to inspire. His sins, and those of the people, are the constant subject of his thoughts; and their forgiveness his constant desire and petition: "Take away," says he, "our iniquities, we beseech Thee, O Lord," that, with a pure mind and heart we may be worthy to enter into the Holy of Holies; for it is not the figurative, but the true Holy of Holies that he is about to enter; it is before something more terrible than the ark of the covenant that he is about to appear; it is not the blood of animals but that of the Son of God, that He is about to offer; he is coming to Jesus, the mediator of the New Testament, the sprinkling of whose blood speaks better things than the blood of Abel.

Arrived at the altar, and bowing down before it, he kisses it out of respect for the spot on which the Divine Victim is about to become present, and in honour of the holy martyrs and saints, whose relics are there deposited, and says: "We "entreat Thee, O God, by the merits of the "saints, whose relics are here present, and of all "the saints, that Thou wouldst forgive us our "sins." It is with good reason that he recommends himself to the prayers of the saints in general, and to those of the martyrs in particular; for the merits of the former, and the blood of the latter, united with the blood of Christ, are of infinite value, and their powerful intercession is most efficacious in obtaining from God the forgiveness of our sins, and all kinds of graces.

From the dawn of Christianity, it has ever been the practice of the Church to offer up the holy sacrifice on the tombs of the martyrs; nay, the tombs of the martyrs were the first altars of Christianity: hence altars to this day are frequently constructed in the shape of tombs. The spots on which the martyrs laid down their lives for Christ, and which imbibed their sacred blood, which they consecrated by the sacrifice of their lives to God, on which they bore a bloody testimony to the divinity of Christ, and to the truth of His religion, have always received special honours from the Church. Hence sacred edifices have been raised over them, which are called *Confessions;* because they there confessed Christ by the sacrifice of their lives. It was there that, on the anniversary of their triumphs, the faithful ever met to offer up the blood of the Lamb slain from the beginning of the world; in order to animate themselves, by the example of the martyrs, to fidelity to their religion, and to implore their intercession; for the voice of the blood of martyrs speaks volumes: "they, being dead, yet speak." (Heb. xi. 4.)

Hence the custom, universally established throughout Christendom, of having relics of saints in the altars. Hence the allusion in the Apocalypse, (vi. 9-11.) "I beheld under the altar the "souls of them that were slain for the love of "God, and the testimony which they held; and "they cried with a loud voice, saying : How long, "O Lord, holy and true, dost Thou not judge, "and revenge our blood on them that dwell on "the earth? And white robes were given to "every one of them; and it was said to them "that they should rest for a little time, till the "number of their brethren, that were also to be "slain for the faith, even as they had been, should "be filled up."

Instructive Subdivision.

This part contains the Introit, the Kyrie, the Gloria, the Collect, the Epistle, the Gospel, and the Creed. The Church has, in this part, joined with instruction the praise of the Almighty, and prayer, in order to prepare the people for the celebration of the awful mysteries, and that their minds and hearts might be filled with holy thoughts and desires.

THE INTROIT

Is one of those parts of the Mass which give it a special character, according to the day or season of the year, the subject of the office of the day being therein proposed, which is either a mystery of the life or death of Christ, or the virtues of a saint, which the Church proposes for our imitation; for the sacrifice of the Mass is offered to God alone, and under no circumstance is it or can it be offered to any saint.

The word *introit* means entrance; for this part is properly the commencement of the Mass. Formerly the Introit consisted of a whole Psalm, which was sung while the faithful were assembling for divine service. At present a verse and anthem only are repeated, together with the doxology. The priest begins with the sign of the cross, as this is the commencement of the Mass, the former prayers being merely introductory.

The ascent of the priest to the altar represents the coming of the Son of God upon earth; and the Introit expresses the longing desires of the ancient just for the coming of the Desired of all nations; to express those desires the words of David are chosen, for He, to use the words of Christ Himself, is "one of the kings and prophets "who so much desired to see the things that you "see, and to hear the things that you hear." More fortunate than those holy personages, the children of the Catholic Church express their joy by hailing the coming of the Redeemer: they possess Him whom the patriarchs, prophets, kings, priests, and all the ancient just desired, and for whose coming they longed, saying: "*Send,* "*O Lord, the Lamb that is to rule us. Come,* "*O Lord, and do not delay.*" (Isaias lx.) During the Introit, we should unite our hearts and desires to those of the ancient just, and endeavour to enter into their dispositions and ardent desires for the establishment of the reign of Christ in our souls; for this is an indispensable disposition to derive benefit from the august sacrifice. What would be the dispositions of Abraham, Isaac, and David, if, like us, they had the happiness of assisting in the Mass at the immolation of the Lamb, whose coming they so ardently desired?

There is a particular Introit for all Sundays and for all the great festivals of the Church. On saints' days, the Introit is generally taken from the office common to all the saints of the same class —whether martyrs, confessors, or virgins, but with some exceptions in favour of particular saints, who were distinguished for some great virtue, or prominent in some great work of faith and charity. Thus, for instance, St. Francis of Assisium, so distinguished for his devotion to the Passion of Christ, and for his zeal in propagating it, has for his Introit those words of St. Paul: "God forbid "that I should glory save in the cross of our Lord "Jesus Christ." (Galatians vi.) St. Lawrence, so renowned on account of his great charity to the poor, has the words of the Psalmist: "He hath "distributed; he hath given to the poor," &c. St. Jerome Æmilian, famed for his compassion on destitute little children, has those words of the Lamentations for his Introit: "My heart "is poured out upon the earth, for the de-"struction of the daughter of my people, when "the children and the sucklings fainted in the "streets of the city." In the Mass for the festival of St. Ignatius of Loyola, the Introit is, "In the "name of Jesus, let every knee bow in heaven, on "earth, and under the earth, and let every tongue "confess that our Lord Jesus Christ is in the "glory of God the Father." St. Camillus, so renowned for his charity to the poor and to the dying, has for his Introit: "Blessed is he that "understandeth concerning the needy and the "poor. The Lord will deliver him in the needy "day, and help him on the bed of sorrow." (Psalm xl.) St. Vincent de Paul, who embraced every kind of good works, and provided asylums for every species of human misery, has for his Introit: "The just man shall flourish like the "palm tree, and grow up like the cedars of the "Libanon." (Isaias xxxv.) Lastly, the Introit for the Mass of St. Aloysius, is: "Thou hast, O "God, made him little inferior to the angels: "Thou hast crowned him with honour and glory." (Psalm viii.)

THE KYRIE ELEISON.

"Have mercy upon me, O God, according to Thy "great mercy, and according to the multitude of Thy "tender mercies blot out my iniquities. Heal me, for I "am infirm and weak." (Psalm l.)

This is an earnest supplication for mercy, suitable to the commencement of so sacred an action as the offering up of the Holy Sacrifice. There is something very striking and beautiful in the amount of penitential and supplicatory addresses thrown into the earlier part of the Liturgy of the Mass.

This short emphatic prayer, "*Have mercy*

"*on us,*" is a cry of the heart, proceeding from a feeling conviction of one's own misery, and of the mercy of God. The Cananean woman has taught us the value of this prayer, which she continued to repeat, with so great confidence in Christ, and such sentiments of her own unworthiness, that at last He granted her request. The blind man of Jericho also teaches us the efficacy of this prayer; for the more that silence was sought to be imposed upon him, with the more ardour did he exclaim, "Jesus, son of David, have mercy on "me," till at last Christ restored to him his sight.

The Kyrie was introduced into the Liturgy in behalf of the catechumens, who were under instruction for baptism, and of the public penitents. Moved by the prayers of the former, and by the tears of the latter, the faithful implored the Almighty in their behalf. They prayed for the former, that God would forgive them their offences, enlighten their hearts, and inspire them with His fear and love; and for the latter, that God would forgive them their sins, and restore them to His favour. When the Kyrie came to be offered up for all the faithful, the custom was introduced of repeating it nine times, in honour of the nine choirs of angels; three times it is addressed to God the Father, three times to God the Son, and three times to God the Holy Ghost.

We call on *God the Father*, as our Creator, Protector, and Parent. As our *Creator*, who knoweth our miseries, and the infirmity of our nature ; " He knoweth our frame, and remember-"eth that we are dust." (Psalm cii.) As our *Protector*, who knoweth that Satan is continually going about, like a roaring lion, seeking whom he may devour, and that the frail vessel of our heart is in continual danger of losing the precious gift of grace. As our *Father*, a name which is to us, a title of confidence, and to Him, a motive of commiseration.

We call upon *God the Son*, as our High Priest, Victim, and Brother. As our *High Priest*, who, having no sins of His own, for which to solicit pardon, applies the whole fruits of the sacrifice for the remission of our sins; and who took upon Him our transgressions, in order, with His infinite sanctity, to make full atonement for them. As our *Victim*, in whom are united, in a sovereign degree, all the properties of propitiation, and expiation, of recovery of favours lost, and of thanksgiving for benefits received. As our *Brother*, to whom we may look up with confidence, since He has taken upon Him our nature, that He might make us His co-heirs.

We call upon *God the Holy Ghost*, as the Author of grace, the Inspirer of prayer, the Sanctifier of souls, our Counsellor, and our Guide.

GLORIA IN EXCELSIS DEO.

"Bless the Lord, O my soul, and let all that is within me praise His holy name." (Psalm cii.)

Immediately after the Kyrie, the priest, standing at the middle of the altar, with his hands extended in the attitude of prayer, and raised up to the height of his shoulders, thereby signifying his love of heavenly things, and his desire of possessing them, commences the *Gloria in excelsis Deo:* at the word *Deo*, he joins his hands and bows, through respect for the name of God. The " Gloria in excelsis" dates from the very origin of Christianity. The angels chanted this canticle of love over the crib of the Infant of Bethlehem. The Church has ever continued to repeat it. Such is the origin of the *Gloria in excelsis*. This canticle comes, with the greatest propriety, immediately after the Kyrie eleison ; for in the Kyrie, the Church had cried to God for mercy: full of confidence that she has obtained it, she sounds the hymn of gratitude : borrowing the identical words of the angels, she chants the great mystery of the Incarnation, which constitutes her happiness, her hopes, and her glory: she, at the same time, lauds the Almighty, and solicits His protection.

As one of the heavenly spirits announced to the

shepherds the good tidings, and a multitude of angels sang the hymn of praise, so the priest at the altar intones this canticle, which is taken up by the faithful: "Glory be to God on high, and peace on earth to men of good will," (St. Luke ii. 14.)

The Introit expresses the longing desires of the ancient just for the coming of the Messias: the *Gloria in excelsis* announces the coming of Him who is the object of their desires. The Introit denotes the time that preceded the coming of the Messias: the *Gloria in excelsis* that which follows it.

This hymn is indeed a hymn worthy of angels, which they might sing among those eternal canticles they are incessantly pouring forth to the Lord of Glory. Of all the forms of praise and adoration, by which we attempt to express our homages to the Almighty, it is one of the finest specimens ever composed by man. We cannot read it attentively, without being filled with a high sense of the majesty of God, and of the homage due to Him by all His creatures. Can there be anything more simple and yet more profound than those beautiful words: *" We praise Thee; we "bless Thee; we glorify Thee; we thank Thee for " Thy great glory, O Lord God, heavenly King, " God the Father Almighty"* ?

In these words, we offer Him the highest tribute

of which the mind and heart of man are capable; we proclaim Him to be worthy of all praise, blessings, and thanksgivings, for His own sake alone, as the Almighty King of heaven and earth, and independently of all the favours conferred upon us, the most unworthy of His creatures.

We thank Him for His own great glory, and for having manifested that glory to us. While calling to mind the Three Persons that subsist in the Godhead, we again renew our adoration, and proclaim, " *Thou only art holy, Thou only art the* " *Lord, Thou only art most high, O Jesus Christ,* " *together with the Holy Ghost, in the glory of* " *God the Father.*"

Between these two parts, which form the beginning and end of this hymn, there are a few words of supplication, in which we call upon the Lamb of God to hear our prayers, and to forgive us our sins: " Who takest away the sins of the " world, have mercy on us," &c.; " receive our prayers."

If ever the Deity condescends to allow creatures so insignificant as we are, to pronounce His praises; if ever He listens to the feeble voice of man, it must be when he uses such accents as these, so worthy of the God whom they celebrate.

Let us, then, in future, make our hearts and minds to correspond with these noble words of our lips, and endeavour to repeat this hymn, with all the devotion which the angels felt when they first sang it. Let us pronounce this hymn with as much respect as if the angels themselves were present, repeating it with us.

The priest concludes the *Gloria in excelsis*, by making on himself the sign of the cross. We cannot too often have recourse to this all-powerful sign, to recall to our minds that all blessings are derived from the cross of Christ. The Church, ever careful to keep up all the holy practices of primitive Christianity, repeats this salutary sign no fewer than seven times during the Mass; at the commencement thereof, at the end of the Gloria, of the Credo, and of the Pater noster, before the two Gospels, and at the end of the Sanctus.

The canticle of angels has resounded; the peace brought upon earth by Christ has been announced. What, then, can be more natural than that the priest should wish it to the faithful? How will he do it?

DOMINUS VOBISCUM.

"The Lord is with thee." (St. Luke, i. 28.)

The Gloria being ended, the priest kisses the altar, and turning towards the people with extended arms, salutes them with these words: "*The*

Lord be with you." The people answer, by returning him the same earnest wish: *"And with thy spirit."* What greater blessings can he impart us, than to have the Lord always with us? If we have Him, we possess all things; without Him, nothing will avail us. When, therefore, you hear the priest pronouncing these words, call to mind the vast importance of their meaning. He prays that the Lord may accompany you wherever you go; that He may be present with you in every place; may protect you in every danger; may guide you, by His watchful providence, unto every good; that He may be with you in the midst of temptations, to enable you to overcome them; in your doubts and difficulties, to counsel you; in your prosperity, to make you use it well; in your adversity, to soften down its asperity, and to strengthen you with patience. "For there is no sanctity if God "withdraws His hand; no wisdom avails if He "cease to govern us; no strength is of any help, "if He support us not; no chastity is secure "without His protection; no guard that we can "keep upon ourselves will profit, if God's holy "Providence watch not over us."—à Kempis, book 3, ch. 14.

As immediately applied to the sacrifice the *Dominus Vobiscum* means that the Lord may be with you during the time of Mass; that He may be constantly in your minds and hearts, and keep you recollected; that He may fill you with a lively faith, and with a spirit of compunction, fervour, and prayer, that you may worthily assist at the holy sacrifice.

We should ever pray that God would be always with us. Can there be a greater happiness than to have Him with us? Thus, we read what God said to the Patriarch Jacob: "I "will be thy keeper, whithersoever thou goest." God was with the Patriarch Joseph in Putiphar's house, and made all that he did to prosper. Putiphar soon perceived that God was with Joseph, and he intrusted the whole of his household and of his affairs to him. "God went down "with him into the dungeon, and left him not till "He brought him the sceptre of the kingdom of "Egypt." Again, God said to Josue: "As I "have been with Moses, so I will be with thee." Again, "Saul was afraid of David; for he saw "that in all things he acted prudently, and that "God was with him."

On the contrary, can there be a greater misfortune, a greater unhappiness, than to be forsaken and cast off by God? "*Woe to them,*" says God, "*when I shall have departed from them,*" (Ozeas ix.) by abandoning them to a hardened and reprobate sense. Those, thus abandoned by God, go on from sin to sin, till at last they are precipitated into eternal flames. This is fully illustrated in the miserable end to which King Saul came, after that God cast him off, for his disobedience to His commands. "Saul's time "was now approaching. The Philistines, whom "he had defeated in the early part of his reign, "when God was with him, were gathering their "armies against Israel, and Saul began to be "dismayed; for he knew that the Lord had "forsaken him, and would not answer him, either "by dreams, by priest, or by prophet. In his "forlorn state he sought refuge in witchcraft. "Samuel, when brought up by the witch, said "to him: 'Why hast thou disturbed my rest, "that I should be brought up?' And Saul "said: 'I am in great distress; for the Philis- "tines fight against me, and God has departed "from me, and will not hear me, either by "the hands of prophets, or by dreams; therefore "I have called thee, that thou mayest show me "what I should do.' Samuel said: 'The Lord "hath indeed departed from thee, and gone over "to thy rival. He will rend thy kingdom out of "thy hands, and will give it to thy rival David: "because thou didst not obey the voice of the "Lord. Therefore, hath the Lord done to thee "what thou sufferest this day. Tomorrow, thou "and thy sons shall be with me in death. And "the Lord will deliver the army of Israel into "the hands of the Philistines." Frightened by these words of Samuel, Saul fell forthwith to the ground; there was no strength in him, for through distress of mind, he had eaten no bread all that day: he was obliged to receive food from the hands of the witch. The next day, Israel fled before the Philistines. Saul's three sons were slain in battle; he himself perished by his own hands, to avoid falling into the hands of the enemy.

Let us, then, never cease praying that God would always keep His hand over us. Let it be our perpetual care that God may be ever with us, to be the soul of our souls, the life of our lives, the will of our wills, the reason of our reason, and to have the whole control of all that regards us. Let us ever pray that He would guide us in all our ways, enlighten us in all our doubts, encourage us in all our difficulties, discover to us all snares, defend us in all dangers, strengthen us against all enemies, and preserve us from the ways of all corruption. This blessing of "*Dominus vobiscum*" is imparted eight times during the divine service.

Bishops, instead of here, like the Priests, addressing the faithful with "*Dominus vobiscum*," greet them with these words: " Pax vobis—Peace be unto you." It was with these words that our Saviour, after His resurrection, saluted His apostles. He had, by His death, made peace between His Eternal Father and mankind, proved by His resurrection that He had made it, and then wished them a share in it.

THE COLLECT.

"When two or three are gathered together in My name, I am in the midst of them." (Matt. xviii. 20.)

"If you ask the Father anything in My name, He will give it you." (St. John xvi. 23.)

The priest now goes to the Epistle corner of the altar, and says aloud: *Oremus*: (*Let us pray.*) This is the second time since the commencement of the Mass, that he has given himself and the people this essential warning. It is repeated five times during the service: after the *Confiteor;* before the *Collect;* before the *Offertory;* before the *Pater noster;* and before the *Post Communion.*

Having invoked the Lord to be with him, to enable him to pray; having warned the people to join with him in prayer, the priest commences the *Collect*, or prayer for the day. This prayer is for two reasons called the *Collect:* 1. Because it is offered up for all present; 2. Because it is an abridgment of all that the priest should ask for himself and for the people. The Collects, for all the Sundays throughout the year, for the great annual solemnities, and for the festivals of the primitive martyrs and saints, were reduced into their present form by the Pontiffs St. Gregory the

Great and Gelasius, while the substance of them is of apostolical origin. They embrace all the subjects for which we ought to pray; and are most worthy of our respect. However varied our wants, our legitimate desires, and our sufferings, they are all fully expressed in these admirable prayers. A particular simplicity and fervour, not to be found elsewhere, reigns throughout them. The Catholic Church alone could compose such prayers. She alone, as the true spouse of Christ, knows how to address Him, and to make an impression on Him.

In penitential seasons, several collects are offered up during the same service. On great solemnities, there is never more than one collect, in order that the whole attention of the people may be concentrated on the particular mystery of the day. However different those mysteries, they all have but one and the same object, the glory of God, and the salvation of man. The Church wishes us to understand, that to ask of God the application of the mystery of the day, is to ask of Him all our wants.

On festivals of saints, the Church, in order to engage us to imitate their examples, makes particular allusion to the principal virtues by which these friends of God were distinguished.

The Collects are always addressed to God the Father, because it is to Him that the sacrifice is offered. They conclude with these words, "*through Christ our Lord.*" This means, that it is *in* Christ, and *through* Christ, that all prayers are addressed to the Eternal Father; there being no mediator between Him and mankind except the Saviour, Jesus. These words also mean that Jesus Christ has not only undertaken to make satisfaction for man's sins, but also to present to His Eternal Father our vows and supplications for mercy, grace, and salvation. This conclusion, lastly, means, that all graces are granted in view of the merits of Jesus Christ. As our Divine Intercessor offers Himself up a victim on our altars, and as we offer Him, in exchange for all the graces that we ask, this formula should inspire us with the greatest confidence. By asking in the name of Christ, we have a right to obtain all our just wishes. May we be convinced of this, while offering up the Collect with the priest.

The assistants answer *Amen* to all the prayers offered up by the priest. This word is a short and energetic acclamation, which means: *we desire what you ask, we join with you in asking it.* Pronounced after the Creed, *Amen* means, *it is true, we believe it.*

The heavenly Jerusalem continually resounds with the word *Amen*, in approbation of the praises of God, sung by the heavenly spirits. Let us endeavour to pronounce it, in the same spirit, that the Church upon earth may more or less resemble that of heaven.

THE EPISTLE.

"All scripture inspired of God, is profitable to teach, "to reprove, to correct, to instruct in justice."—2 Timothy iii. 16.

"God, at sundry times, and in divers manners, spoke "in times past to the fathers by the prophets."— Hebrews i.

"The holy men of God spoke, inspired by the Holy "Ghost."—2 Peter i.

When we pray, we speak to God: God speaks to us, when we read His holy word. Having already spoken to God in the different prayers which the Church enjoins, and, above all, in that prayer, (the Collect,) which the priest, with his hands extended towards heaven, offers, in the name of the united assembly of the faithful, then it is that the Supreme Majesty of Heaven condescends to bend down from the skies to speak to us, and to offer us instructions suitable to our particular wants and necessities. Let us, therefore, listen to the instructions which it contains, with that holy avidity which a hunger and thirst after justice inspires. Let us, at the same time, remember that if the word of God does not prove the means of our correction in time, it will certainly rise to our condemnation in eternity; for it will not return to God without effect, either as our reward or as our condemnation. To this purpose are those words of our Lord, to certain Jews : " Those who are of God, listen to the words " of God ; but you do not listen to them, because "you are not of God." (St. John viii. 47.) One principal object of public worship is, to enlighten and strengthen our faith, to teach us what we are to believe and to practise, " for without faith it " is impossible to please God ;" " faith comes by " hearing, and hearing by the word of Christ." (Rom. x. 17.) "And faith without works is dead in itself." (St. James ii. 26.) Hence St. Paul says : " Give attention to reading, meditating on " these things, that thy proficiency may be mani-" fest to all." (1 Timothy iv.)

The apostles, while engaged in propagating and establishing Christianity, could not remain long in one place, but were continually passing from country to country. In their solicitude to enlighten and confirm in the faith the converts they had made, they frequently wrote to the different Churches they had founded, Epistles, full of heavenly wisdom and doctrine, and suitable to their spiritual wants. They commanded them to be read, not only to the faithful to whom they were addressed, but also in all the surrounding churches. These Epistles were received with the greatest veneration, being inspired by the Holy Ghost, and were preserved with the utmost care. The bishops made it their duty to expound and inculcate their contents. Hence the universal custom of reading during divine service, a portion of the letters of the apostles, especially of those of St. Paul. We should listen to the reading of them, as if SS. Peter, Paul, or John were actually speaking to us; for it is their very words that then resound in our ears, as they resounded in the ears of our ancestors in the faith.

We should pray that they would make on our minds and hearts the same impressions they made on the minds and hearts of the primitive Christians. We should listen to the reading of them in the spirit of prayer, which solicits the ability to comprehend these divine precepts, and the facility to practise them. Not content with listening to the word of God read in the temple, we should, on our return to our respective homes, peruse it again, that, being the more impressed with the truths it contains, we may the more feelingly enter into the spirit of it, and derive more abundant graces from it.

To St. Jerome do we owe the selection of the portions of the Epistles and Gospels that are publicly read on Sundays, and on the principal festivals, in our churches; which selection was adopted by Pope St. Damasus.

It was from the Roman Church, the mother

and mistress of all churches, that all the national churches of Christendom received this selection.

It is not without good reason, that the Epistle is read before the Gospel; for thus, the voice of the prophets, and of the apostles, prepares us to listen to a voice still more holy, to that of the Son of God Himself, the Master of the prophets and of the apostles. During His public life He sent the Baptist, and His apostles, two and two, to prepare His ways. The Introit, and the Epistle, are, as it were, the dawn of the morn, which precedes the brilliant rays of the rising Sun of the Gospel.

THE GOSPEL.

"Last of all, in these days, God has spoken to us by "His Son, by whom He created all things." (Heb. i.)

The custom of reading to the assembled faithful a portion of the Gospel on Sundays and holy-days, commenced immediately after the Gospel was committed to writing. What indeed can be more necessary than that they who assist at the sacrifice of Christ, should be fully instructed in His doctrine, in His precepts, and in His actions, and should publicly testify their respect and love for them?

The Gospel is read at the corner of the altar opposite to that at which the Epistle was read, in order to represent the passing from the old to the new covenant of God with mankind. While passin to the Gospel corner of the altar, the priest bows down before the middle thereof, and, reflecting how unworthy his lips are to utter divine oracles, he begs of the Almighty to purify both his heart and his lips, as He once did, with a burning coal, the lips of the Prophet Isaiah; and thus enable him worthily to announce His Gospel.

"All Scripture, being divinely inspired," is the word of God, and, as such, is entitled to our respect; yet a distinction is properly observed between the Gospel of Christ and the writings of the apostles; for the former emanated immediately from the very lips of the God-Man Himself, and therefore a more marked attention is due to it. Hence, when the priest arrives at the Gospel corner of the altar, the whole congregation, through respect for the word of God, and to show their readiness to follow Christ, stands up simultaneously, to listen to the reading of it in that respectful posture. In the ages of faith, at the reading of the Gospel, the Knights of Malta, as also, the once gallant Polish nobility, drew their swords from their scabbards, and stood in a military attitude, thereby testifying their readiness to shed their blood in defence of Christianity. History, which records their noble deeds of valour, is there to attest that this was no mere vain idle ceremony.

While pronouncing the name of the Evangelist, of whose Gospel a portion is about to be read, the priest and the people make the sign of the cross on their foreheads, on their mouths, and on their breasts. We are thus reminded of the great blessings conferred on us by our Saviour's passion, which are unfolded in the sacred volume, a portion of which is about to be read. We sign our foreheads with the sign of the cross, to show that we are not ashamed of Christ's doctrine; we sign our mouths with it, to show that we will never deny it; and our breasts, to show that we entertain a sincere attachment and affection for it in our hearts, and that we will ever make it the rule of our conduct. The clerk then answers, *Glory be to God!* Yes, glory be to God, who has called us out of the darkness of ignorance into His admirable light, and who has enlightened us with the knowledge of His truth, and pointed out to us the paths of justice and of salvation; for in those portions of Scripture that are read to us we find examples to imitate, mysteries to exercise our faith, promises to entertain our hopes, rules to direct our conduct, threats to restrain us from sin, and grace to make us love and practise what they prescribe. Let us, then, listen to them with awe, veneration, docility, confidence, and fidelity. With the same act of praise, which marked the commencement of the

Gospel, does it also terminate: *Praise be to Thee, O Christ.* Never was praise better bestowed. What are we of ourselves? Captives of Satan, exiles from heaven, travellers passing through the desert of this life, this valley of tears. What is the Gospel? Good news: to captives, the good news of their deliverance; to exiles, permission to return to their native country and homes; to weary and anxious travellers, news that a safe and charitable guide has descended from heaven to lead and guide them thither. Were we fully sensible of what we should still be without the Gospel, what we were before we knew it, and what we should again become without it; with what deep sense of gratitude should we repeat, *Praise be to Thee, O Christ.* Praise and Glory to Christ, the Saviour of the world! Let us beg of God that, as we firmly believe in the Gospel of Christ, so we may faithfully live up to it.

THE CREED.

"With the heart, we believe unto justification; but "with the mouth, confession is made unto salvation."—Rom. x. 10.

"Without faith, it is impossible to please God. He "that cometh to God must believe that He is, and is a "rewarder of them that seek Him."—Heb. xi. 6.

The Mass being a complete homage offered to God, a full profession of our faith should be embodied therein; for God requires of us by faith to humble our understandings to His word, as we humble our bodies to Him by our external homage, and submit our actions to Him, by regulating them according to His commandments.

Christ died for all men, "*that whosoever believ-*" "*eth in Him, may not perish, but have eternal*" "*life.*" (St. John iii.) The Church being the interpreter of His word, we are all obliged to adopt her interpretation thereof, under penalty of being regarded as heathens and publicans. (St. Matt. xviii. 17.) The creed is a summary of the doctrine which she proposes to our belief. The Creed here repeated is the Nicene Creed, drawn up A.D. 325. The Apostles' Creed is but a short account, almost without commentary, of the life of Christ, an abridgment of the instructions which the primitive converts received before baptism. This Creed was sufficient while the primitive Christians were all practice, and knew not how to dispute about religion, but to live according to it, and to die for God. They did not then talk great things; but honoured God, and preached to their neighbours by their good conduct; in a word, they lived the Gospel. But when the charity of many grew cold, when some refused to submit their understandings to the yoke of faith, the Church, which Christ had commissioned to teach all nations, and with which He had promised to abide for ever, in order to preserve in its purity the deposit of faith, to reduce every height that exalted itself against the knowledge of God, and to bring into captivity every understanding to the obedience of Christ, the Church, I say, placed in their true and full light the mysteries of faith; and in so doing, made several additions to the Apostles' Creed. Hence the three other Creeds, are but the Apostles' Creed, together with the explanations made by the Church at different periods, in condemnation of the successively rising heresies.

Thus, relatively to God the Father, the Church, in opposition to the Manichean heresy, which admitted two creative principles, a good and a bad one, inserted in the Creed the words, "*I believe in one God, the Almighty, maker of all things, visible and invisible.*"

On the divinity of Christ, the Apostles' Creed has only, "*and in Jesus Christ, His only Son, our Lord:*" whereas, the Church, in condemnation of the Arian heresy, which denied the Divinity of Christ, has added: "*And in one Lord Jesus Christ, the only-begotten Son of God, born of the Father before all ages; God of God; Light of Light; True God of True God; begotten, not made; consubstantial to the Father, by whom all things were made.*"

And on the Divinity of the Holy Ghost, the

Apostles' Creed has only, "*I believe in the Holy Ghost:*" whereas, the Church, in condemnation of the heresy of Macedonius, who denied the Divinity of the Holy Ghost, the Third Person of the Holy Trinity, has inserted in the Creed: "*And in the Holy Ghost, the Lord and Giver of Life, who proceedeth from the Father and the Son; who, together with the Father and the Son, is adored and glorified; who spoke by the prophets.*"

The faith which we profess is always the same, whichever of the three formularies we recite, that of the Apostles, of Nicea, or of Saint Athanasius. In each of these we shall find the same mysteries, and we should profess them with the same sentiments of faith and veneration. Let this declaration, "*I believe,*" be ever on our lips, but more especially let it be engraven on our hearts; and let us resolve to make our actions correspond with our professions.

The Creed terminates with these words: "*I believe in the life of the world to come.*" Yes, I believe in a future life; I expect it with all the fervour of hope. I demand it with all the energy that the Spirit of God can inspire; I will dispose myself for the possession thereof with all the zeal and fidelity that the grace of God can form in my heart: till admitted into the realms of the blessed, I will never cease to repeat here below the *Amen* which is expressive of the most ardent desire thereof.

At the moment that the mystery of the Incarnation is announced, all kneel to honour by this act of humiliation the profound humility of Jesus Christ; for a God who is humble should be approached only in humility. How great is the sacrifice which a God was pleased to make in order to secure our freedom from the bondage of sin. An humbled God, should be approached not only with apparent, but also with sincere humility. He to whom all nature is subject condescends to become a man of poverty; He who was descended from the Kings of Judah, and was established the King of Nations, condescended to become a man unknown and of nought; He who had never by sin merited death, became mortal, to deliver us from slavery and restore us to liberty.

It is not a barren faith with which the Church seeks to inspire us, by commanding us to make this public profession of our faith. In order to be profitable, our faith must be *firm*, not doubting or hesitating; for it cannot have a stronger foundation than the veracity of God, upon which all the articles of faith are grounded : it must be *universal*, embracing every article, for they are all equally the word of God; it must be in our *hearts ;* we must have a great respect for all its objects, for there is no part of our religion but which deserves our veneration. Our faith must be *lively*, manifesting itself in all our actions, for unless our lives be better than the lives of those who have no faith, our condemnation will undoubtedly be much greater. Let us never, therefore, separate the faith of our minds from the practice of our lives. Let us cherish this precious gift with which God has favoured us, by always aspiring after Him who is the great object thereof: we must show our faith in our *words*, by always speaking respectfully of religion, and of everything belonging to it ; in our *conduct*, by avoiding all those whose conversation would tend to weaken our faith, which ought to be the chief ornament and honour of our lives: "for the *just man lives by faith.*" In a word, we are to be totally guided by the precepts of that faith which was given us to be our chief consolation here, and the effectual means of conducting us to an uninterrupted bliss hereafter, when faith shall be swallowed up in reality.

On Sundays and holy days of obligation, the reading of the Gospel is followed by an instruction on some article of the Creed, on one of the commandments, or on one of the sacraments; lest that "the little ones should ask for bread, and that "there should be none to break it unto them." (Lamentations iv. 4.)

SECOND ARTICLE.

PREPARATION OF THE MATTER OF THE SACRIFICE.

This part of the Liturgy greatly rises in importance over the preceding. This is properly the commencement of the Sacrifice. The prayers and lessons which I have hitherto endeavoured to explain are merely of a preparatory nature. This is the moment in which the Church really begins to act, and to offer the Victim. This may, in some degree, be considered an essential part of the Sacrifice. The nearer we approach the essential act of the Sacrifice, the more interesting does the matter become, and consequently, a renewal of attention and devotion is here necessary.

An offering up to God of the matter or victim of the sacrifice is an essential part thereof. But this is not that offering; this is but a preparatory offering; for as yet it is only bread and wine, and therefore of value only from what it will become when changed by the words of consecration into the Body and Blood of Christ.

OFFERTORY.

"In a contrite and humble heart let us be accepted." —Daniel iii. 39.

The principal disposition which this part of the Sacrifice requires is that of a contrite and humble heart. The Church here particularly directs our attention to this twofold disposition, in order that this oblation, which of its nature is necessarily acceptable to God, it being His only-begotten Son who here humbles Himself in presence of His Eternal Father, may become profitable to us, by the union of our dispositions with those of our Divine Saviour.

But in order fully to understand the particular nature of the Sacrifice of the Mass, it is necessary to know, who is the chief priest thereof, to whom is the offering made, what is the nature of the offering, and for what end it is offered.

1. Who is the Chief Priest or offerer of the Sacrifice of the Mass.—The principal offerer thereof is no other than Jesus Christ. He alone is the eternal priest "according to the order of "Melchisedech;" (Psalm cix.) the High Priest of the good things to come, who, having no sins of His own to expiate, is fully entitled to offer sacrifice for the sins of mankind. In consideration of the honour due to His Divine Person, and

of His obedience to His Eternal Father unto death, this sacrifice is sure of finding acceptance, for He here renews, by the hands of the priest, those august functions which He is continually performing in heaven, offering His precious Body as a ransom for sin, and His precious Blood to efface the stains of our souls. Hence we say in our manuals: "We offer to Thee, O God, by the "hands of our High Priest, Jesus Christ Thy "Son, the Sacrifice of His Body and Blood, in "union with the Sacrifice He once offered to Thee "on the cross."

2. The *Church, through* and *with* Jesus Christ, offers up this sacrifice. In consequence of the union of the Church with Christ, of whom she is the mystical body, she cooperates with Him in whatever He does, and through Him, has a right to present to the Eternal Father a living, holy, and unpolluted Victim.

3. The visible priest offers up this Sacrifice in *the name of the Church;* for he is anointed and consecrated with holy oil for the performance of this awful function. The Almighty is graciously pleased to consider his hands, as those of the Church, or of Jesus Christ Himself.

4. and lastly.—The faithful offer it up by the hands of the priest, in the name of the Church, and through the merits of Jesus Christ. Hence we read in our manuals: "Accept, O God, this

"offering made to Thee by Thy minister, in the "name of all present, and of Thy whole Church, "triumphant, militant, and suffering in Purga-"tory."

II. To whom is the offering of the Sacrifice of the Mass made?—It is made to the Eternal Father, in memory of the Passion, Resurrection, and Ascension of our Lord and Saviour Jesus Christ, and to the adorable Trinity, as an homage to atone for the outrage offered to it by sin, and as a thanksgiving for the inestimable benefit of our justification.

III. Who is it that is offered?—It is Jesus Christ, who is a true Holocaust, a Victim of propitiation for sin, a Victim of thanksgiving, a Victim of pacification; in a word, He in whom every species of oblation is comprised, and who, by this single oblation, consummates the eternal sanctification of the whole world.

IV. What are the motives of this Sacrifice?—The bread and wine are first successively offered up, and afterwards simultaneously or conjointly.

The bread and wine are first offered up *successively* for the four great ends of sacrifice. The offering of them is also made in the name of all present, both priest and people, and of the whole Church of Christ; for the living and for the dead; for the just and for sinners; for all their necessities, spiritual and temporal; that all may obtain pardon of their sins, offences, and negligences; and beseeching the Divine Majesty, that the offering may ascend before His clemency as a sweet odour for the salvation of all.

These motives are expressed in the two separate oblations of the bread and wine.

The bread and wine are afterwards conjointly offered up, in compliance with the Divine command, in commemoration of our Saviour's Passion, Resurrection, and Ascension.

The Oblation, like all the other parts of the Mass, commences with prayer; for the Church considers the fruit of all her religious exercises to be dependent on prayer. Hence the priest says aloud, " *Let us pray.*" He at the same time elevates the Host upon the paten, raises his eyes towards Heaven, where God has fixed the throne of His glory, where the Victim of universal efficacy offers a perpetual sacrifice to His Eternal Father, and whence both the benediction which is to consecrate the Host, and the sacred fire which is to consume the Victim, are to descend. He afterwards lowers his looks towards the Host, because it does not become man to fix an indiscreet and presumptuous look upon God, and God admonishes him to look into himself, to consider his miseries and bewail his offences.

Let us, then, transport ourselves in spirit to that most important moment when Jesus Christ, after having taken the bread into His hands, and rendered thanks to His Eternal Father, took also the wine and blessed it, assuring His apostles that He would drink no more of the fruit of the vine till He had entered His kingdom.

While making the Oblation, the priest secretly recites the following prayer of oblation: "Accept, "O Holy Father, Almighty Eternal God, this im-"maculate Host, which I, Thy unworthy servant, "offer Thee, my living and true God, for my "innumerable sins, offences, and negligences, for "all now present, moreover for all faithful "Christians, living and dead, that it may be "profitable for my own and for their salvation "unto eternal life. Amen."

Before depositing the Host and the chalice on the altar, he makes the sign of the cross with each of them, to signify that the oblation derives all its efficacy from the Cross and Passion of our Redeemer.

THE MIXTURE OF THE WINE AND WATER.

He, at the Epistle corner of the altar, then pours into the chalice the wine for consecration, mixing with it a small quantity of water, and saying: "*O God, who didst wonderfully form the "substance of man, and yet more wonderfully re-"generate it, grant us, by the mystery of this wine "and water, to be united with His divinity, who*

"*deigned to become partaker of our humanity,*
"*Thy Son Jesus Christ our Lord.*"

It is by order of the Church, on the strength of a most ancient, and, as it is supposed, an apostolical tradition, that the water is added to the wine. This practice is symbolical of the Incarnation; the wine, as the more precious element, representing the Divinity of Christ; the water, as inferior, representing His sacred humanity. We are here reminded of the whole history of man, of his creation in a state of perfection, of his fall and degradation, of Satan's victory over him, and of his restoration and sanctification by Jesus Christ.

Having returned to the middle of the altar, holding up the chalice, and looking up to the crucifix, he pronounces the prayer of oblation:
"*We offer Thee, O Lord, the chalice of salvation,*
"*beseeching Thy clemency, that it may ascend in*
"*the sight of Thy Divine Majesty with the odour*
"*of sweetness for our salvation, and for the salva-*
"*tion of the whole world. Amen.*"

This noble prayer, to use the words of Tertullian, declares Jesus Christ to be the universal priest of His Eternal Father; His blood having purified heaven and earth : "for He is the Vic-"tim of propitiation for our sins, and not only "for ours, but for those of the whole world." (1 St. John ii. 2.)

After this prayer, he, with the chalice, makes the sign of the cross on the altar, thereby showing that he places the offering on the cross of Jesus Christ.

But, fearing lest his unworthiness should render the sacrifice less agreeable to God, he bows down, and, with hands joined, and placed on the edge of the altar, he, in the attitude of supplication, repeats, in the name of the assistants, that humble prayer offered up by the three Israelitish youths, at Babylon, previously to their being cast into the fiery furnace. (Daniel iii. 39.) "In the spirit of humility, and in a contrite and humble "heart, grant us, O Lord, to be received by "Thee; and let this our sacrifice be so made in "Thy sight, that it may please Thee, O Lord "God."

Raising, then, up towards heaven his hands, and immediately lowering them, thereby invoking the Holy Ghost, the Spirit of Fire, the Sanctifying Spirit, which occasionally consumed the ancient holocausts, and which now daily consumes our offerings in a miraculous manner, he prays: "Come, O Sanctifier, Almighty Eternal God, and "bless this sacrifice, prepared for the glory of Thy "holy name." At the word *bless*, he makes the sign of the cross over the chalice and over the host, to give to understand, that it is through the Sacrifice of the Cross that he looks for the coming of the Holy Ghost, to change the bread and wine into the Body and Blood of Jesus Christ.

He again moves to the Epistle corner of the altar, where he washes the tips of his fingers in a small vessel prepared for that purpose. The symbolical meaning of this action is, to remind him of the purity required of those who come before God at His altar. This practice is of apostolical tradition, originating in the custom of the Jews, who frequently washed their hands during their sacrifices. The latter part of the twenty-fifth Psalm, which is then repeated, is singularly appropriate, both to the act of washing, and to the purity which the Sacrifice demands. Observe, that in all the preceding prayers, the minister has, either in his own name, or in that of the people, always acknowledged himself a sinner, incessantly solicited mercy and indulgence, and washed the extremities of his fingers, lest that, notwithstanding all his precautions, some secret weakness may still lurk behind, unknown and unrepented of.

CONTINUATION OF THE OBLATION—SIMULTANEOUS OBLATION OF THE BREAD AND WINE.

"*Suscipe sancta Trinitas,*" &c.

Having offered up, in the name of the Church, the bread and wine, and the faithful having also offered them with him, to recognize the supreme dominion of God over them, and to expiate their sins, the priest returns to the middle of the altar, bows down and makes to the Holy Trinity another oblation, expressing, at the same time, his object in so doing. He had above made a separate oblation of the bread and wine; he now makes a simultaneous oblation of them both, in memory of the mysteries of Christ's Death, Resurrection, and Ascension, and in honour of the saints; that is to say, to thank God for the favours conferred by Him on them, and to merit their protection. "*Receive,*" says he, "*O Holy Trinity, this obla-
"tion which we make Thee, in memory of the
"Passion, Resurrection, and Ascension of our
"Lord Jesus Christ; in honour of the Blessed
"Mary ever a Virgin, of Blessed John the Bap-
"tist, and of the holy apostles Saints Peter and
"Paul, of these, and of all the saints; that it
"may avail to their honour, and to our salvation;
"that they, whose memory we celebrate on earth,
"may vouchsafe to pray for us in heaven. Through
"the same Christ our Lord.*"

This prayer reminds us that it is as an everlasting memorial of Christ's Passion, Resurrection, and Ascension, that we frequent the holy Sacrifice of the Mass; and that we celebrate on earth the memory of the saints, that they may obtain mercy for us through Jesus Christ, before the throne of God in heaven.

This prayer contains, though in a different degree, the names of all those who have any right to the sacrifice. First, God the Father, to whom the Sacrifice is offered: Jesus Christ, who, as the Victim thereof, is offered in memory of His Passion, Resurrection, and Ascension; and consequently, as raised up before the throne of God, to be always present before Him, to plead our cause. The Church of heaven, as also that of earth, are mentioned, because they join in partaking of the universal sacrifice. The Church on earth partakes sacramentally thereof, and thence derives additional benefits. The Church triumphant also partakes thereof, in an invisible manner, by the communication of the glorious life of Jesus Christ.

While offering up this prayer, the priest bows down, with his hands joined on the edge of the altar, thereby acknowledging himself unworthy to offer to the Almighty this great sacrifice, and to show how innocent one should be to appear before God on the part of mankind.

ORATE FRATRES.

"Pray for us; pray for one another that you may be saved."—Hebrews xiii. 18.; St. James v. 16.

Prayer is the duty of every Christian, and the very essence of spiritual life. The grace of God, which animates and supports us in a course of holiness, is but the effect of prayer, bestowed upon us by the Almighty. A Christian ought not to confine his prayers to his own personal necessities: the Church, which prays for all, wishes all her children to unite in one common prayer for their common necessities. To this, she exhorts them in the words of the text: "*Pray for one "another.*"

She considers salvation as the reward, not only of him who is the object of the prayer, but also of him who prays, and of that charity which teaches us to sympathise in the miseries of our brethren, as though they were our own.

The priest kisses the altar, which is an emblem of Jesus Christ, in order thence to draw those holy dispositions, of the necessity of which he is more and more convinced. In order to obtain them for the faithful, He turns towards them and addresses them, extending his arms, as if wishing to embrace them, saying, "*Pray, my brethren, "that this my sacrifice and yours may prove* "*acceptable to God the Father Almighty.*" "*May the Lord,*" replies the congregation, "*May the Lord receive this sacrifice from thy hands, to the praise and glory of His name, to our benefit, and to that of all His holy Church.*"

Pray, for our mutual interests are here nearly concerned. *Brethren,* you are my brethren in Jesus Christ. This sacrifice is my sacrifice and yours. It is my sacrifice, since I have been established in the ministry thereof. It is also yours, in a sense, indeed, less extensive, but not the less real. I am about to offer it through Jesus Christ, while you are about to offer it with Him, and by my hands. It is of the utmost importance that this sacrifice should *prove acceptable to God the Father.*

For God, who is great, powerful, and just, may behold such injustices in our hands, such criminal desires in our hearts, and such stains on our consciences, as to render us unworthy to participate in the fruits of this sacrifice; and it is with a view to engage you to enter into fresh sentiments of grief and sorrow for our mutual offences, that I here renew my solicitations to you to pray.

To an invitation so justly made, and so beneficial in its consequences, the faithful reply: Yes, we pray, we demand with all the ardour of our souls, that *thy God and ours may receive this sacrifice from thy hands.* We beseech the

Almighty that thy hands may be effectually raised towards heaven, as well for us as for yourself. We will never forget that the primary object of this sacrifice is to make due reparation to the Almighty, for the glory of which we have defrauded Him by our sins. *May this sacrifice be conducive to our benefit.* May its efficacy extend to all our necessities, and purify our souls; may it shed the light of wisdom upon our minds, inflame our hearts, and guide our steps. Let us not, at the same time, lose sight of the general interests of *His holy Church.*

It is to God the Father that the sacrifice is about to be presented. Jesus Christ, our Brother, is to be the offerer thereof. It is to be offered by a minister chosen from amongst us; and it was for the sanctification of all mankind that this tremendous mystery, which is about to be renewed, was originally consummated.

The principal motive of the prayer *Orate Fratres* is, that the nearer we approach the moment of the sacrifice, the more necessary do prayer and recollection become.

The priest will not again turn round to the people till the sacrifice is accomplished, and the communion received. The reason is, because he is now entering upon the more solemn part of the Mass, which includes the consecration and communion; and which therefore requires his whole attention, that must not henceforth be distracted by turning away from this sacred object. When, therefore, the priest turns to the people for the last time, at the *Orate Fratres*, you may consider him as taking leave of you, and entering, as the High Priest formerly did, into the Holy of Holies. Hitherto he has prayed like one of yourselves, standing in the midst of you, speaking and praying aloud, that you might join with him. With you and for you, he made the confession of his sins; gave praise to God at the *Gloria;* read the Epistle and Gospel for your instruction; joined, at the Creed, in one profession of faith: but now he separates from the people. Like Moses, he leaves us at the foot of the mount, while he ascends to the summit to converse with God alone.

THE SECRET

Is one or more prayers, which always correspond in number and subject with the Collect, commemorate the same solemnity, or beg the intercession of the same saint, as was mentioned in the Collect.

THE PREFACE.

" Thou art worthy, O Lord our God, to receive glory
" and honour, and power, because Thou hast created
" all things, and for Thy will they have been created.
" The Lamb that was slain is worthy to receive power,
" and divinity, and wisdom, and strength, and honour,
" and glory, and benediction."—Apocalypse iv. 11; v. 12.

As we advance in the Liturgy of the Mass, the dignity and importance of the subject increases at each step. The Preface is an introduction to the sacred Canon, or action of the sacrifice, which is the most solemn part of the whole Mass.

After the *Orate Fratres*, we beheld the priest quitting the people, and bidding them, as it were, a solemn adieu, by recommending himself to their prayers; we observed that he entered the Holy of Holies, not to return thence till the mystery of our redemption should be consummated. Accordingly, in the Greek and Oriental churches a curtain is then let to fall, which divides the sanctuary from the body of the church; and in the Western Church it was formerly the custom to close the gates of the sanctuary before the Preface, in order to announce the absence and separation of the priest from the rest of the faithful, which is requisite, while he is wrapt in holy communion with God, and honoured with His most intimate communications.

The Preface is a sublime and affecting form of

adoration, praise, and thanksgiving; made to God through Jesus Christ our mediator; in which we intreat the supreme Lord of heaven and earth to permit us to join our voices with those of the angelic choirs in proclaiming His eternal praises.

Still, from the hallowed recesses of the sanctuary, the priest addresses the people in the most pathetic strains and exhortations. This reminds us of the mystery of Jesus Christ at the same time present in heaven and on earth; on earth to instruct and animate us, in heaven to protect and defend us. Let us, therefore, attend to him with docility when he solicits our prayers.

The words: "*Per omnia secula sæculorum,*" are the last words of the conclusion of the *Secret* prayer, or prayers, and mean "*for ever and ever.*" The conclusion of the *Secret* is as follows: " Through Christ our Lord, who with the Father " and the Son, liveth throughout all ages. Amen." The priest raises his voice at the last words, "*per* "*omnia sæcula sæculorum,*" that the faithful may join in and sanction the petition contained in the *Secret* prayer. This shows that the people should join with the priest in this prayer, and ask of God the same graces.

He then pronounces the benediction, *Dominus Vobiscum,* which he has already so often bestowed; ·but, being no longer considered as in the midst of them, he does not turn round towards them;

but pronounces in a voice sufficiently audible, "*Dominus Vobiscum—The Lord be with you.*"

Raising up, then, his hands from the altar, he thus addresses the people: "*Lift up your hearts:*" as if to say: "Withdraw them entirely from "earth; put yourselves in communion with the "angels in heaven, that we may worthily together "prepare for the coming of the Lord." The people, in the person of the minister, respond, "*Our hearts are already lifted up, and with the* "*Lord.*"

If ever there be a time when our minds, so bent down to this earth, should raise themselves from all its groveling concerns, and aspire to heaven, it is surely at the time of prayer, and in the hour of sacrifice, when we are told to ascend in spirit, and join the heavenly choirs in singing the praises of our great Creator.

The priest proceeds: "*Let us give thanks to the* "*Lord our God.*" Let us thank Him for all His benefits, especially for the eucharistic sacrifice. To this the clerk, in the name of the people, answers: "*It is right and just that we should do* "*so.*" *It is right*, on account of the manifold blessings we receive from Him; and *just*, for thanksgiving is the least return we can in justice make to God for all His favours.

The priest here begins the Preface, by echoing the pious sentiment of the response, and repeating

it with increased force. "*It is truly right and
"*salutary.*" To being proper and just, he adds
motives of our own interest: "*it is available to
"salvation, that we should always, and in all
"places, give thanks to Thee.*" Accordingly, the
Psalmist (Psalm cii.) bids us to bless the Lord
in every place, and at all times, and that His
praise should always be in our mouths.

"*O holy Lord, Almighty Father, eternal God.*"
Yes, we owe Him adoration as our Sovereign
Lord and God, who is full of sanctity, and who
exists for ever and ever, and as our Father, who
is all-powerful, and willing to assist us His children.

But, however just it is that we should adore,
thank, and praise Him, our homage will not be
accepted, unless offered "*through Jesus Christ our
Lord.*" For He is our mediator with God.
"Him we have for our advocate with the Father;
"and by Him we have access, through faith, into
"this grace, wherein we stand." (Rom. v. 2.) He
is God by nature, and man by obedience; at
once our Lord, and sovereign ruler of heaven and
earth. He holds the middle space between the
city of the living God, and the terrestrial Jerusalem.

"*By whom the angels praise Thy majesty, the
"dominations adore it, the powers tremble before*

"*it, the heavens, the heavenly virtues and blessed seraphim with common jubilee glorify it.*"

A principal point of view, in which the Preface is entitled to our particular consideration is, that the great object of it is to unite the Church militant on earth with the Church triumphant in heaven, in praising God. The priest here prays in the name of the faithful as well as of himself: "*In union with whom* (the angels) *we beseech Thee, that Thou wouldst command our voices also to be admitted, with suppliant confession,*" &c.

The Church here prays that our voices may be joined with those of the holy angels, who are now actually assisting at the great sacrifice, and preparing to commend it to the acceptance of the Eternal Father. It is Jesus Christ that gives utterance to our tongues that we may give praise to His Eternal Father; and it is also through Him that all the Heavenly Host render their homage to the Divine Majesty, according to the varied ranks which it has pleased Him to assign them. As, then, we are permitted to join our voices with those of the blessed spirits in rendering a grateful homage to our common Lord, we ought to endeavour to resemble them as nearly as possible in the fervour of their charity, and to copy their obedience and fidelity, that we may be found worthy of being associated with them in their canticles of everlasting praise.

The *Sanctus* is a hymn which earth owes to heaven, which the Church triumphant in heaven has sent to the Church militant on earth, that the latter may learn to repeat it in the place of her exile, hoping that her members may one day join with them in singing it in the regions of bliss. The Prophet Isaias heard the seraphim in heaven repeating it; and St. John declares that the heavenly Jerusalem continually resounds with it.

While repeating the *Sanctus* the priest lowers his voice, to excite attention; but still continues it in an audible tone, that the faithful may join with him in repeating it. While repeating this canticle he bows down, with hands joined.

A bell is then rung, to give warning that the priest is about to commence the Canon, during which the consecration is to be effected. Hosanna is an energetic exclamation, like Amen and Alleluia. It was with those words, "*Hosanna in the "highest; Blessed is he that cometh in the name "of the Lord; Hosanna in the highest!*" that the children of Jerusalem saluted our Lord on His triumphant entry into Jerusalem. They are here most appropriate, as our Lord is about to become present on our altars. The priest makes the sign of the cross upon himself, to intimate that the action by which Christ is about to be rendered present, is representative of the sacrifice of the Cross.

The Sanctus and Benedictus constitute the gist of the Preface: all that precedes is but a preparation or introduction to them. It is in order to this, that we may worthily join the angels in singing these hymns, that at the commencement of the Preface the priest warns the faithful to raise up their hearts towards heaven.

The disposition of holy awe is necessary to make us recite these hymns with effect; for as the angels while chanting them veil their countenances with their wings, so does the priest in repeating them join his hands and bow down in profound adoration. It is to a thrice-holy God that our homages are addressed. Let, then, every word of this canticle recall to our minds the obligation which His holiness imposes upon us of endeavouring to imitate Him. Hence God Himself says, "*Be ye holy, as I am holy.*" (1 Peter i. 16.)

THIRD ARTICLE,

OR DIVISION OF THE LITURGY OF THE MASS.

THE CANON.

"From the rising of the sun, even till the going down "thereof, My name is great among the Gentiles, and in "every place there is sacrifice, and there is offered to "My name a clean oblation. For My name is great "among the Gentiles, saith the Lord of Hosts."—Mal. i. 11.

The parts of the Mass which I have hitherto explained, although most holy prayers and exercises, form no essential part of the sacrifice, being only immediate preparations for it. We are now come to the very action of the Sacrifice, as this part of the Liturgy is sometimes called.

It is commonly called the *Canon*, or fixed rule of prayers, by which the Sacrifice is commanded by the Church to be offered up: it never varies on any day of the year throughout the whole Catholic Church. It extends to the Lord's Prayer, and contains all the prayers that accompany the action of the Sacrifice, together with the different applications of the merits thereof, and of the intentions with which it is offered up.

The Canon consists of the very words of our

Lord Himself, of the traditions of the Apostles, and of the ordinances of primitive martyred popes. Its containing no names but those of the apostles and primitive martyrs, shows that it is prior in date to the fourth century of Christianity. Saints Gregory the Great and Leo the Great, are the last popes that have made any addition to the canon, and these are inconsiderable ones.

Wherever the Church extends her authority, every minister is subjected to the same essential order of prayer, without being at liberty either to add to or to retrench anything from the formulas and ceremonies there prescribed. It has always been, and ever will be, considered the most excellent of all prayers, the Lord's prayer excepted, that which imparts a value to all other prayers, inasmuch as it is, of all others, the most intimately connected with the sacrifice of Jesus Christ. No period can be assigned in which the Holy Sacrifice was offered up under any other form of prayers. The Universal Church has at all times offered up to God the same supplications, and observed the same rites and ceremonies.

The priest, during the whole time of the Canon, holds his hands in an elevated posture, expressive of the elevation of his and our hearts to heaven. This should serve to remind us, that we must make the most vigorous efforts to resist the spirit of dissipation, so inimical to attention and fervour. It is, therefore, of the utmost importance fully to understand the prayers that compose the Canon of the Mass, that we may be feelingly impressed with the sentiments they breathe.

THE FIRST PRAYER OF THE CANON—TE IGITUR.

"Then shalt Thou accept the sacrifice of justice, ''oblations, and burnt-offerings."—Psalm L

The Canon commences with a prayer for the Church, and for those by whom it is guided and protected. We demand, in the first place, that the fruits of this Sacrifice, may be applied to the whole Catholic Church. She alone possesses the right to participate therein, and to impart its blessings to those who are attached to her unity. She is the Church of God; she is His household; she alone can in some measure be truly said to partake of the immensity of God. It is for her principally that the Sacrifice is offered up; that it may please the Almighty to grant her peace, by keeping her under His protection, by enlightening her with His wisdom, and animating her with His charity. It is He who governs her throughout the whole world, by presiding at the instructions of her ministers.

Since, in order to produce these effects, she stands in need of a visible head, partaking of the sanctity of Him who is her invisible head, we pray for the Vicar of Jesus Christ on earth, the successor of the blessed Apostle St. Peter, who is the rock upon which His Church is built, that he may be in the midst of the Church a vigilant sentinel to guard her.

This prayer embraces the interests of the whole Christian Church. For the same reason, we pray for the bishop to whose care providence has, in a more particular manner, intrusted us. Protected by those whom God has given the Church for her rulers, she requires the support also of her members.

No one is forgotten in this prayer. We pray for all mankind, but particularly for those whom God has united with us in the same holy faith. For, though we ought to love and esteem every human creature without exception, we may and ought to have a particular regard for all whose faith is orthodox—that is, conformable to the doctrine of the universal Church, and who profess with us the Catholic and apostolical faith : all these have an especial claim to a share in the general supplication, and are entitled to the benefits of the Sacrifice.

SECOND PRAYER OF THE CANON—MEMENTO OF THE LIVING.

"Pray for one another."—St. James v. 16.

To this general prayer for the whole Church we immediately add a particular prayer for our friends, called the *Memento of the Living*, because we, at present, name only our living friends; another part of the Mass being appropriated for the remembrance of the dead.

To pray for one another is a general duty of all Christians. To some this duty is doubly urgent; for when any favour, spiritual or temporal, has been conferred upon us, there arises an obligation of making a grateful return by praying for our benefactors, especially if it be out of our power to make them any other recompense. This is an exercise of the most tender and affectionate nature, to commend, in the ardour of our devotion, to the divine protection the names of all those who are most dear to us. It is here the priest particularly prays for those for whom he offers up the Mass; then for all those for whom he is bound by particular motives of justice and gratitude to pray; namely, his benefactors, and his spiritual children, whose difficulties, temptations, or spiritual wants, are particularly known to him. We here pray also for our relations.

On this occasion, the Church has adopted the prayer of the good thief upon the cross. "*Re-member me*," said he, "*when Thou comest into Thy kingdom.*" So we now pray: "*Remember, O Lord, Thy servants, both men and women, and all here present, whose faith is known and their devotion manifest to Thee; for whom we offer up to Thee, or who offer, this sacrifice of praise; for themselves and all theirs; for the redemption of their souls, for the hope of their salvation and safety, and who render their vows to Thee, the eternal living and true God.*"

The words *remember*, or, *be mindful, O Lord*, is only an expression accommodated to our manner of speaking. Unlike the children of men, God is not subject to forgetfulness; every creature is constantly in His presence; this mindfulness on His part, merely consists in affording us sensible testimonies of His attention, and in pouring forth His graces and blessings upon us His poor and needy creatures. All that we demand by this form of address to the Almighty is, that He would give us a sensible proof that our prayers are not rejected. "*Both men and women.*" These words merely serve to remind the priest of the different necessities of those whom he recommends.

"*Remember,*" or "*be mindful,*" continues the

priest, "*of all here present;*" for, independently of the general right which all the members of the Catholic Church have to partake of this oblation in quality of children of the Church, those present have a special right to the prayers of the priest, to whom they are united by the oblation, and with whom they may in some sense be said to offer it up; but at the same time that he makes this prayer in their behalf, he gives them a lesson in the following words: "*whose faith and devotion are known to Thee, O God;*" by reminding them that these prayers are only conditional, and that he has no intention to pray, except for those who approach this sacrifice with a pure faith, and with sentiments of true devotion, "*for the redemption of their souls, and for the hope of their salvation and safety.*"

Those words show that this prayer is not confined to the mere mention of the faithful, who offer, or for whom the sacrifice is offered; it embraces everything that regards them; he therefore solicits the redemption of their souls, through the pardon of all their offences; he prays for their perseverance in the ways of salvation, by their being supported in the midst of the perils by which they are surrounded, with the cheering hope of salvation; he even solicits their preservation in health, and an exemption from all the ills that trouble the peace and happiness of life.

This prayer likewise extends to all those to whom the faithful are united by the ties of blood or friendship, or connected by the relations and duties of society; *for we pray for themselves and for theirs:* namely, their children, relatives, friends, domestic inferiors, and all those whom Providence has entrusted to their charge, because each of those relations imposes its particular duties, and requires those particular graces which can only be demanded through Jesus Christ, and obtained by the merits of His sacrifice.

Let us, therefore, banish from our hearts every feeling contrary to the purity of this sacrifice; let us endeavour to render the prayers, which the priest of Jesus Christ offers up in our behalf, worthy of the Victim who presents them, and worthy of obtaining for us, and for all those who are dear to us, the blessings of life eternal, together with the graces that are proper to conduct us thither. Amen.

THIRD PRAYER OF THE CANON.—INFRA ACTIONEM.

The meaning of this title is this: The priest, having specified for whom he is to offer the holy sacrifice, now enters upon the most solemn part of it, called the *action*, which commences with the commemoration of the saints in glory. Hence the three next prayers which precede the consecration, and the three that follow it, are said to be within the action of the Sacrifice, or *infra actionem*, or *intra actionem*.

THIRD PRAYER OF THE CANON— COMMUNICANTES, &c.

"I will save Jerusalem for My own sake, and for the "sake of My servant David."—4 Kings xix. 34.

The communion of saints, by which the Church on earth forms but one body with that of heaven, separated indeed at present by time and place, but destined for a perfect union in eternity, is an article of our creed, which exalts the dignity of man, fills him with hope, and cheers him up in the difficult passages of life. This dogma is here considered inasmuch only as it regards the right which the saints in heaven have to our homage, and that which faith gives us to their protection. An article, of so much importance, is with great propriety introduced into the prayers of that Sacrifice which forms the subject of their adoration as well as ours.

Having, by our prayers, done what we could for the welfare of the Church on earth, we are now anxious to secure the prayers of the members of the same Church, who, having completed the time of their probation here on earth, are now enjoying their reward in heaven.

The following are the words of this prayer: "*Communicating with, and venerating the memory of, the glorious and ever blessed Virgin Mary, Mother of God, of the twelve apostles, of the martyrs, and of all the saints, by whose prayers and merits grant, O God, that in all things we may be armed with the help of Thy protection, through the same Jesus Christ our Lord.*"

1. "*Communicating with,*" that is, joining with, claiming and asserting our privilege and honour, as members of the true Church, of which Christ is the Head, equally with the saints in heaven, who are our elder brethren; with them we join in the common homage we both offer to the Creator of all things; for our Sacrifice is theirs also. Hence we read in our manuals: "We join our hearts and voices with all the "blessed in heaven, and with Thy whole Church "on earth; we come to offer Thee with them our "homages; we desire with them to adore, praise, "and glorify Thee, and to give Thee thanks for "Thy great glory."

2. *We venerate the memories of the saints.*— "It is," says St. Augustine, "a great honour to "be named in the presence of our Lord, whilst we "celebrate His death in this awful sacrifice." At this offering, each class of saints has its particular commendation. 1. The Mother of our Lord stands supereminent above all the saints, in considera-

tion that the blood which is about to flow on our altars, is that of her Son. After her, there are none more venerable than the apostles, who learnt from the mouth of Christ Himself, the value of the sacrifice we are about to offer.

And what can be more just than that an honourable mention should be made of the martyrs during the august Sacrifice? Their blood mingled with that of the Lamb, has been accepted as a perfect holocaust. They have a peculiar claim to our veneration, since they laid down their lives to transmit to us the precious deposit intrusted to their care.

3. In order to make us enter more feelingly into the spirit of the communion of saints, the Church advances one step beyond commemoration, and authorizes us to invoke them especially as they owe their own salvation to the efficacy of this Sacrifice. Hence the priest prays: "*By whose merits and "prayers, grant, O God, that we may be always "defended by the help of Thy protection, through "Jesus Christ our Lord.*" What is it that we demand of the saints but that, through their intercession, we may be always defended by the Almighty, and enjoy the blessing of His protection; and that the angels would fill their censers with the sweet perfume of the prayers of the saints, and make it ascend before God in our behalf. (Apoc. viii. 4.) The help of the saints

is but the protection of the Almighty Himself, who is the sole object of our vows and desires. To God alone we attribute that foresight which foresees all our necessities, and that omnipotence which sustains us under all our trials; all that we ask of the friends of God is, that by the help of their prayers, we may be made partakers of the Divine mercy, and enjoy the aid of His protection. But, as the saints derive all their influence from Jesus Christ, it is through this divine Saviour that we pray that their merits may prove effectual in our regard.

Hence we say in our Manuals that through Jesus Christ we hope to be one day admitted into the company of all the saints and elect, with whom we here on earth communicate in these holy mysteries, whose memories we celebrate, and whose prayers we desire.

FOURTH PRAYER OF THE CANON.—HANC IGITUR, &c.

"The priest shall put his hand upon the head of the victim, and it shall be acceptable, and help to expiation."—Leviticus i. 4.

In the preceding prayer, the Church on earth entered into communion with the Church in heaven. The two sisters joined in order to offer up the great sacrifice which rejoices them both. The priest is their minister. He is about to take possession of the victim in their name. Behold him extending his hands over the host and chalice. This imposing ceremony carries us back three thousand years. It reminds us of Aaron, and his successors in the priesthood, spreading their hands on the head of the victim, thereby taking possession of it on the part of God, and declaring that the animal whose blood was about to flow, was substituted to suffer in their own place, they being guilty and deserving of death.

But it is no longer on the figurative victim that the priest spreads his hands, but on the true victim which has been expected during four thousand years. His hands, like Aaron's, proclaim that it is he himself that is guilty, and who should be sacrificed in the stead of the innocent victim. With what awe should we not be seized when we behold this august ceremony, and hear the words by which the holiness of God is invoked to take possession of the victim: " *We entreat* " *Thee, O Lord, favourably to receive this obla-* " *tion, in acknowledgment of our servitude; to* " *dispose our days in Thy peace; to preserve us* " *from eternal damnation, and to reckon us among* " *the number of Thy elect. Through Jesus Christ* " *our Lord. Amen.*"

The first prayer of the Canon commenced thus: " *We therefore humbly pray and beseech Thee.*"

We now read: "*We therefore beseech Thee, O Lord, graciously to accept this oblation;*" to remind us that the application of the merits of this sacrifice can be obtained only by prayer.

It is termed the *oblation of our servitude,* because it is a service, a duty, an obligation incumbent on us, to offer up sacrifice to God. The priest here speaks in his own name; for he is not the less obliged to acknowledge his dependance on God, than the faithful, and the offering he makes of the Body and Blood of Christ is an act of this acknowledgment. The faithful, who are ransomed by the Blood of a God, are also consequently bound to serve Him who has paid this infinite price for their ransom. It is with a view constantly to keep us in mind of the sovereign dominion of God over His creatures, and of the Redeemer over the souls which He has purchased, that the Church has ordained this sacrifice to be offered up as a homage of our servitude.

It is also the homage and the *oblation of Thy whole family.*—Of Thy Church, which Thou hast brought forth upon the cross. It is the offering which she presents to Thee in token of her dependance, her gratitude, and her love. This oblation embraces every one that belongs to her; all who profess the same faith, immolate the same Victim, unite in the same prayers, and solicit the same benedictions. Should this sacrifice be offered up in the remotest corner of the earth; should the minister be surrounded but by a handful of her children, still it would be the offering of God's whole family.

This whole family, with united voice, solicits three great favours, which include every other that the heart of man can desire. First, That He would dispose our days in His peace; would enable us to pass our days in peace and harmony with one another; and, above all, give us that interior peace of mind which arises from the testimony of a good conscience, which He alone can give. Secondly, That He would deliver us from eternal damnation, and, as a prelude to it, that He would preserve us from mortal sin, which alone can expose us to damnation; and, finally, that He would number us among the flock of His elect. This will form the completion of all our happiness, the object which we strive to obtain by all our prayers and exertions in the service of God.

Thus, peace in this world, exemption from sin, and everlasting salvation are the advantages we hope for from this sacrifice, all of which we express in the above prayer. Let us ask them with confidence. The Blood of the Second Abel is all powerful to obtain them for us.

FIFTH PRAYER OF THE CANON, WHICH IMMEDIATELY PRECEDES THE CONSECRATION—QUAM OBLATIONEM.

"God spoke, and all things were made."—Psalm xxxii. 9.

It is the same God who now, at the moment of the Consecration, is about to speak, and whose word is about to produce effects infinitely more astonishing than the creation of the world, and of all the wonders it contains. Let us listen to what the ancient holy fathers have taught on this subject.

Although the prayer *Quam oblationem*, which is derived from tradition, can bear no comparison with the words of Christ, which are destined to operate the greatest of our mysteries, yet it has so intimate and indispensable a connection with this mystery, and with the words by which it is effected, that the holy fathers in all ages have not hesitated to regard it as forming a part of the consecration: not that the Church attributes to these words, which she has joined to those of the consecration, the same virtue as to those of Jesus Christ. It is an article of faith, that the substances of bread and wine are not changed till the priest has pronounced the words of Christ; but it is essential to the sacrifice, that the intention of the Church, which offers them, should be manifested. The august sacrifice cannot be validly offered up unless the intentions of the offering priest are conformable to those of Jesus Christ, our principal High Priest and Victim; now in the words of this prayer, the sentiments of the Church are clearly and determinately expressed. As, therefore, it is correct to say that the words, "*This is My Body: This is My Blood,*" operate the mystery, so it is equally correct to say, that the words which compose the prayer *Quam oblationem* are preparatory to it.

The priest begins this prayer with his hands joined before his breast, and separates them only to make *three* signs of the cross, first, over the entire oblation, and afterwards a separate sign on each of the substances of the bread and wine. These signs of the cross show that the sacrifice of the Mass derives all its efficacy from the sacrifice of the Cross. They have for their particular object to draw down on the bread and wine the virtue and efficacy of the Sacrifice of the Cross. The nearer the moment approaches, when the Victim is to be offered in an unbloody manner, the more reason has the priest to employ this sign which tends so strongly to remind us of the oblation heretofore made in a bloody manner. An explanation of this prayer will convince us of this important truth.

"*Which oblation, we beseech Thee, O Lord, that Thou wouldst vouchsafe to make in all things blessed, approved, ratified, rational, and acceptable, that it may become to us the Body and Blood of Thy most beloved Son Jesus Christ.*" Is it possible for so great a mystery to be expressed in fewer words?

"*Do Thou vouchsafe.*"—Do Thou who art God, what is best pleasing to Thy divine majesty, Who, as the source of all justice, dost desire the abolition of sin and the re-establishment of justice; Who, as bounty itself, desirest that the sinner should be justified and live: we present to Thee, this bread and wine, because Thy Son has chosen them, and this choice has rendered them precious gifts, and exalted them to the dignity of a pure and spotless oblation; Thou hast chosen them as a means to shed abroad Thy most abundant benedictions; for the blessings conferred by them comprehend every kind of benediction, the germ of all graces, and the principle of all benedictions; they being capable of fulfilling all our desires, relieving all our necessities, and of enabling us to satisfy all our obligations.

"*May it be made for us the Body and Blood of Thy most Beloved Son Jesus Christ;*" in the presence of the angels who adore, of the saints who glorify, of the Church which invokes, of the ministers who offer, and of the faithful who expect it with a holy ardour; may God, who condescends to operate this prodigy in our behalf, find nothing henceforward in our hearts repugnant to the character of well-beloved children, associated with Jesus Christ.

We are now about to fix the eyes of our faith on the words of consecration. What preparation of mind and heart is on our part requisite to meditate worthily on subjects of such importance! Religion, however enlightened in her dogmas, and sublime in her mysteries, has nothing so august and so holy as this to offer us, since the words which we are about to contemplate contain the principle of true happiness in time, and the germ of unfading bliss in eternity.

THE CONSECRATION.

"This is My Body; This is My Blood."—St. Matt. xxvi. 26, 28.

We come now to the action of the sacrifice or consecration. This is, properly, the only *action* in all religion. There is not a prayer or benediction in all religion, but what derives from it all its merit and value. It is also called the *Consecration* on account of the change which Jesus Christ makes of these elements into His Body and Blood, by which they become a pure, holy, perfect, reasonable, and acceptable Victim, which, from its very nature, cannot fail to appease the justice, honour the wisdom, second the mercy, and correspond with the dignity of the Godhead. In order to give us to understand that we can never approach this solemn action with too great a degree of preparation, nor with too high an idea of its importance, the Church has placed the consecration in the centre of all her prayers. As every part of the Liturgy preceding the Consecration has served to announce its excellence, and inspire us with the holiest dispositions, so every prayer that follows it, tends to apply the fruit thereof, and to warm our hearts with gratitude.

Moreover, as the Consecration itself is placed in the centre of the prayers of the Liturgy, so in like manner are the words of consecration placed in the midst of an abridged recital of the circumstances that accompanied the institution of this great mystery. "Who, the day before He suf-
"fered, took bread into His holy and venerable
"hands, and, with His eyes lifted up towards
"heaven, giving thanks to Thee, Almighty God,
"His Father, He blessed, broke, and gave it to
"His disciples, saying," &c.

"Represent to yourselves," says St. Chrysostom, (De Sacerdotio,) "the Prophet Elias praying
"prostrate on the ground, before the victim
"placed upon the altar, and surrounded by a vast
"multitude of people awaiting in solemn expecta-

"tion and silence for the fire of heaven to descend
"and consume the Victim. This is awful. But
"what is it compared to what takes place on our
"altars at the moment of consecration! It is no
"longer the fire of heaven, but the God of heaven
"whom the priest, like the prophet, is about to call
"down." At the moment of the consecration, the
veil, which formerly separated the sanctuary from
the body of the church, was withdrawn, that the
whole congregation might intimately unite themselves to this adorable mystery. In the churches
where the veil is not used, the sound of a bell
announces to all present, that the greatest of mysteries is about to be accomplished. "At the voice
"of the priest," says St. Gregory the Great, "the
"heavens are opened; the angels become present;
"earthly things are joined to heavenly things,
"and visible and invisible things become one!"

Calling to mind the great mysteries of faith,
arming himself with that sublime power with
which he was invested at his ordination, in the
name and person of Christ, whose words the
priest uses, or rather whose organ he becomes,
he lifts up his eyes towards heaven, and, giving
thanks to his Eternal Father, blesses the bread
and says,—"Take ye and eat, *for This is My
Body.*"

In like manner, taking the chalice into his
hands, he blesses it, and says :—" Drink ye all of

"this. *This is the chalice of My Blood of the new
"testament, which shall be shed for you, and for
"many unto the remission of sins.*" (St. Matth.
xxvi. 26-7; St. Luke xxii. 20.) "This is the
"accomplishment of the promise made at Caphar-
"naum: this is the bread which came down from
"heaven; of which, whosoever eateth, shall live
"for ever. This bread is My Flesh, which I shall
"give for the life of the world. *This is the Blood
"of the New Testament or Covenant.*" This is
the blood of a God, shed in honour of a God,
which fully and perfectly atones for all the outrages offered to God. It is the blood of the most
holy and most excellent of the children of men;
which reconciles an offended Father to His rebellious children; which atones for the accumu-
lated outrages of ages, effaces sins of the deepest
dye, and ensures to all pardon, grace, and salvation.

"*This is My Blood.*"—It is no longer Moses
that speaks; it is no longer question of a tempo-
rary covenant, and of a law of death. This covenant, like the former, is cemented with blood, but
not with the blood of a mortal victim destitute of
sense and reason, but with the Blood of a God.
"*It is My Blood,*" said He who had previously
said, "*I come that ye may have life, and may
"have it more abundantly.*"

"*It is the cup of the new and eternal testa-*

"*ment.*" This is the Blood of the true Paschal Lamb, which, as it tinges your lips, will be a signal to the destroying angel to take to flight. This is the Blood which, carried by the supreme High Priest into the sanctuary of heaven, pleads more loudly in our behalf, in accents of mercy and forgiveness, than did that of Abel.

The great miracle is accomplished! The Son of God—the Eternal—the Strong—the Almighty—the Creator of worlds, is become obedient to the voice of a mortal man! By the omnipotent power of God, the bread and wine are instantly changed into the Body and Blood of Jesus Christ. "Look," says St. Chrysostom, "into the interior "of the sanctuary, as into the interior of heaven "itself! Behold with the eyes of faith, Jesus "Christ, there surrounded by an innumerable "multitude of angels, prostrate before Him."

"What," says St. Cyril of Jerusalem, "when "Christ says it is so, will any one be bold enough "to say it is not so? Shall we even presume to "doubt when He so solemnly declares that this is "His Body and Blood?"

Immediately after those words: "*This is My* "*Body—This is My Blood—Do this in remem-* "*brance of Me*"—the priest falls down to adore, and raises up the Host and Chalice, that the faithful may likewise adore them.

"The wise men," says St. Chrysostom, "came

"a long journey to adore this Body, with fear and
"trembling. Let us, who are citizens of heaven,
"imitate those barbarians. For, beholding the
"stable and the manger only, without having
"witnessed the great things which we have wit-
"nessed, and without knowing the great myste-
"ries and truths that we know, they came and
"adored with great reverence. You behold that
"same Body, not in a manger, but on the altar;
"not carried in His mother's arms, but elevated
"in the priest's hands, and under the wings of
"the Holy Ghost, whose gifts are most abun-
"dantly showered down on the Sacrifice. Let us,
"therefore, be roused and tremble; let us bring
"more devotion to the altar, than the Eastern
"Kings did to the manger, where, with a lively
"faith, and with the most profound sentiments
"of religion, they adored their new-born Saviour."

The object of the elevation of the Host and Chalice is, to represent the raising up of the Body of Christ on the Cross; that the faithful may have an opportunity of adoring Jesus Christ under the sacred elements; and of honouring and imitating the profound humiliation of the Son of God, who at this moment prostrates Himself before the majesty of His Eternal Father. Jesus Christ then calls out to us from the altar: "Je suis un Dieu
"très present. Je suis aussi present que lorsqu'
"aux jours de ma vie mortelle, j'accomplissois

"les mystères dont ce sacrifice est l'abrégé: vous "êtes devant l'autel où je m'immole, devant le "trône de ma misericorde, devant ce que le ciel "a de plus saint et de plus grand."

All hail, most blessed Jesus, Son of the Most High God! I adore Thee. Thou art Christ, the Son of the Living God. Thou art the Lamb of God that died on the Cross to save us.

Hail, precious Body, that was nailed to the Cross for our sins! Hail, Sacred Blood, that flowed from the wounds of Jesus to cleanse us from all our sins!

Eternal Father, look down upon this Sacred Victim which was once offered to Thee on the Cross, and is now daily offered to Thee! look not upon our sins, but on the infinite ransom paid for them! Look upon the face of Thy Christ, here present upon the altar, and, through the merits of this adorable Victim, look down upon us in mercy! Accept, O God, of this Divine oblation, and, through the merits of Christ's Passion and Death, be pleased to look upon us, and upon all Thy people, in mercy! Amen.

FIRST PRAYER AFTER THE ELEVATION.

" Do this in remembrance of Me."—Luke xxii. 19.

These words are the title of the power of the priest, and the proof of the mystery which has been just accomplished.

In obedience to this command, "*Do this in* "*remembrance of Me,*" the priest offers up the following prayer: " *Whence, both we Thy ser-* "*vants, also Thy holy people, mindful, O Lord,* " *as well of Thy blessed Passion, as of Thy* " *glorious resurrection from the dead, and of Thy* " *admirable ascension into heaven, do offer to Thy* "*most Holy Majesty, of these Thy gifts and grants,* " *a pure Host, a holy Host, an immaculate Host,* " *the holy Bread of Life Eternal, and the chalice* " *of perpetual salvation.*"

In every sacrifice there must be an offering, it being an essential part of sacrifice. At the Offertory, the simple elements of bread and wine were presented to the Almighty, as a preparatory offering, to receive His blessing. That blessing having been received, and the consecration effected, we have it now in our power to make to God an offering worthy of Him, the essential offering of the Sacrifice, which we present to His Divine Majesty. In conformity with our Saviour's command, we offer it in remembrance of His Passion, Resurrection, and Ascension. *"Do this in re-" "membrance of Me."*

A particular object of the Sacrifice of the Mass being to remind us of the Passion of Christ; the Church reminds us also of the mysteries of Christ's Resurrection and Ascension, because they are necessarily connected with Christ's Passion.

Thus we communicate with Christ *dead,* who by His death has destroyed the empire of death over us, by rendering temporal our death, which would otherwise have been eternal, and by making it the passage to an endless life. We communicate with Christ *risen from the dead,* whose Resurrection is the principle and model of our resurrection. We communicate with Christ *ascended up to heaven,* which makes us desire to ascend with Him.

The priest then makes the sign of the cross five times over the Body and Blood of Christ. There is every difference between the signs of the cross made *after* the consecration and those made *before* it. The object of those made *before* the consecration is to draw down the graces of God on the offerings, and to impress on our minds that it is only through the merits of Christ that we expect them. The signs of the cross made *after* the consecration show that the sacred elements are the real Body and Blood of Christ, and that the

Sacrifice of the Mass is the same as that of the Cross. Accordingly, after the consecration there is no further invocation of the blessing of God.

By those five signs of the cross, the Church wishes more and more to inculcate, and make us sensible that the Victim of the Sacrifice of the Mass is the same as the Victim of Calvary. By those five signs of the cross the priest equivalently says: We offer to Thy supreme majesty this *holy* Host, which was offered on the cross; this *pure* Host, which was attached to the cross; this *spotless* Host, which was immolated on the cross; this *Sacred Bread*, which is Jesus Christ, the living and eternal Bread descended from heaven, who died on the cross to impart life to us; the *Chalice of Salvation*, the Blood of Christ, the mediator of the new alliance, that Blood which was shed on the cross for the redemption of our souls. At those precious and awful moments, the Church wishes that we should be more and more convinced of the actual presence of Christ on our altars, and think of nothing else. Could she better manifest her faith in the miraculous change which has just taken place? Could she more forcibly tell us to behave at the foot of the altar, as if we were present at the foot of the cross itself?

SECOND PRAYER AFTER THE ELEVATION.

"Thou art a priest for ever, according to the order of "Melchisedech." (Heb. v. 6.)

While reminding the Eternal Father that the Sacrifice of Christ is the universal sacrifice, of which the ancient sacrifices were but so many emblems, the Church entreats Him to impart to us the like dispositions, with which the ancient sacrificers were animated, in offering figurative victims, as, the innocence of Abel, the faith of Abraham, and the holiness of Melchisedech.

"*Look down,*" he says, "*with a propitious and serene countenance, upon these offerings, and accept them, as Thou didst accept those of Thy righteous servant Abel, the sacrifice of our father Abraham, and that which Thy high priest Melchisedech offered Thee.*"

God always beholds the Victim with complacency, but our offering of it may not be so acceptable to Him; to remove this obstacle is the object of this prayer. If we have not the innocence and generosity of Abel, the faith and courage of Abraham, nor the holiness of Melchisedech, let us ask these dispositions of God, particularly during this prayer.

THIRD PRAYER AFTER THE ELEVATION.—SUPPLICES
TE ROGAMUS.

"The prayers of the saints ascended from the hand of "the angel before God."—Apoc. viii. 4.

This short prayer is one of the most important of the Mass. It is full of elevated ideas and sublime mysteries. The priest now joins his hands before his breast, bows down, and in this humble posture offers up this prayer. "We most "humbly beseech Thee, Almighty God, to com- "mand these things to be carried by the hands "of Thy holy angel, to Thy altar on high, into "the presence of Thy Divine Majesty, that as "many as partake of this altar, by receiving the "most sacred Body and Blood of Thy Son, may "be filled with all heavenly blessings and graces."

In the first of the three preceding prayers, we offer up to God this Sacrifice; in the second, we entreat Him to accept of it; and in the third, we entreat Him, as the fruits of this oblation, to shower down upon us His choicest graces and blessings.

Who is this holy angel? It is no other than Jesus Christ Himself, who undertakes to present the oblation. The priest entreats Him to carry the Victim before the throne of His Eternal Father in heaven. Through respect for Jesus

Christ, he does not presume to name Him to His Eternal Father. This Angel Mediator being equal to the Eternal Father, is certain of procuring the acceptance of this Sacrifice, which is both His and ours.

We have beheld the Angel of the Lord ascending to the high altar in heaven to present the Host of propitiation. We now behold Him descending towards earth, to shower down upon us those graces and benedictions which are the fruits of this Sacrifice, and as if thus addressing the faithful surrounding the altar : " However varied your " spiritual wants may be, approach with confi- " dence; this Sacrifice is more than sufficient to " supply them all. If you are sinners, solicit " your conversion ; if you are just, pray for your " perseverance in justice ; if tempted, pray for " strength : this Sacrifice is the pledge of all " graces." The signs of the cross here made denote the presence of the holy and divine Victim on the altar of the Church.

Hence we pray in our manuals : " While we " offer this Host here below upon our altars, do " Thou receive it upon Thine altar above, from " the hands of the Angel of great counsel, the " Eternal Priest; and thence send down Thy " blessings upon us all, who here below assist at " Thy divine mysteries : through the same Jesus " Christ our Lord. Amen."

The Church, like a tender mother, is ever anxious that all her children should partake of the treasure of Christ's merits, to which she has free access during the august sacrifice.

Before the consecration she applied the merits of the sacrifice to the whole universal Church, and for those for whom she was particularly bound to apply them. She also invoked the intercession of the saints reigning in heaven in their behalf. After the consecration she first prays for all her children who are no longer in this life; and, lastly, for all present at the holy Sacrifice, for whom, and for himself, the priest solicits their admission into the kingdom of heaven.

FOURTH PRAYER AFTER THE ELEVATION—MEMENTO FOR THE DEAD.

"Have pity on me, you, at least, my friends, for the hand of the Lord hath touched me."—Job xix. 21.

It would be superfluous here to remind good and well-instructed Catholics that the Church, from the time of the apostles, has ever prayed for her departed children, and inculcated the necessity and importance of this duty.

There are some who live so well as not to require this Sacrifice of the Mediator; and there are others that have led such bad lives, that this Sacrifice would profit them nothing. It is only, therefore, for the middle sort, between those two, that prayer is profitable. For these, it has the effect that God treats them with more mercy than their sins would otherwise deserve. In conformity with this doctrine the Canon of the Mass contains the following prayer for the departed friends and members of the Church.

"*Be mindful, O Lord, of Thy servants and handmaids, who have gone before us in the sign of faith, and sleep in the sleep of peace..........*
To them, O Lord, and to all who rest in Christ, we beseech that Thou wouldst grant a place of refreshment, light, and peace, through the same Christ our Lord. Amen."

First, we beg of God to remember in His mercy *all who are gone before us.* Whither are they gone? Not into everlasting darkness; they are not lost: nor yet into their eternal rest; they are not innocent: they are reserved in God's holy keeping, who chastises them in due measure, according to their defects.

They are gone before us. Then we shall follow them: we are separated only for a time; and then, we shall want that help which they now implore from us.

Who are gone before us in the sign of faith.— That is, who, having been baptized, have died in the true faith, and in the peace of God, that is, in a state of grace. We, therefore, exclude from our prayers all who evidently die in a state of mortal sin; such, for instance, who having an opportunity, refuse to receive the rites of the Church, and die out of her communion. We think it useless to pray for such. As for those who die out of the faith of the Catholic Church, there is no law to exclude our charity towards them. We may pray for them *privately*, especially if they have led good lives, and if there be ground to hope that their error was not wilful. Still, the Church forbids their names to be publicly mentioned during divine service after their death, to show her detestation of the guilt of heresy and disobedience.

Who sleep in the sleep of peace.—These souls are not sunk in the depth of death eternal. Compared with it, theirs is justly styled *the sleep of peace.*

The priest then, joining his hands before his breast, prays a few moments for them, and mentions the names of persons for whom he particularly wishes to pray; he again extends his hands, and concludes this prayer in these words: " *To these, O Lord, and to all that rest in* " *Christ, grant, we beseech Thee, a place of* " *refreshment, light, and peace.*"

To these, O Lord, and to all that rest in Christ. —These words show that the Church prays for all the souls detained in Purgatory; that they have a share in the merits of the Sacrifice; and that none are excepted or forgotten, although not named. Grant a *place of refreshment;* for they are yet in pain and suffering; *a place of light,* and rescue them from the darkness in which they are involved; *and a place of peace,* where they shall have no more trouble, no more pain or sorrow; but be perfectly and eternally happy in the enjoyment of God.

The honour of God, charity, justice, and our own interest, oblige us to pray for the dead.

FIFTH PRAYER AFTER THE ELEVATION, AND THE LAST OF THE CANON.—NOBIS QUOQUE PECCATORIBUS.

" If we say that we have no sin, we deceive ourselves, " and the truth is not in us."—1 S. John i. 8.

Having finished our prayer for the dead, who though sinners are yet eternally fixed in the grace of God, which they can never lose, we again turn our thoughts upon ourselves, who are sinners of a very different description, not knowing if we possess the favour of God; and if we do, uncertain whether we shall persevere to the end in this favour. The priest here elevates his voice a little, that he may be better heard in this humble acknowledgment; and, striking his breast in imitation of the publican, he says: "To us sinners also, Thy servants, trusting to "the multitude of Thy mercies, vouchsafe to "grant some part and fellowship with Thy holy "apostles and martyrs, &c., and, with all Thy "saints, into whose company we beseech Thee to "admit us, not in consideration of our merits, but "through Thy gratuitous pardon. Through Jesus "Christ our Lord. Amen."

To us sinners.—These words admonish us that the fruit of this Sacrifice is dependent upon the sincere avowal of our iniquities. To solicit pardon while we treat ourselves with severity, is to honour God's sanctity, to interest His mercy, and to forward the designs of His justice. Let us then with the priest raise the voice of our hearts to confess that we are sinners. The priest strikes his breast, because he considers this avowal, made in the name of the people, equally applicable to himself. We hesitate not to pronounce ourselves *servants of God*, when we reflect on the noble destiny to which He has called us. By nature we are sinners; by grace we are called to be, not only the servants, but even the *children of God*, heirs of heaven, and joint heirs with Jesus Christ and His saints. These considerations elevate our spirits, and make us aspire to the realms above. Thither we immediately raise our minds, and send forth the most ardent wishes that the

Almighty would grant us some part and fellowship with His apostles and martyrs, who are already reigning there, and that He would one day admit us into that blessed company.

The Church, before the Consecration, invoked the saints, in order to give additional weight to her prayers. She now renews her invocation of them. By the former, the Church instructs us to offer the sacrifice in union with the saints; by the latter, she invites us to render ourselves worthy of sharing in their glory. In the one, the Church names the apostles, and those who, after their example, have contributed to establish and support religion by their labours, and who defended it by their sufferings; in the other, she mentions those who, in the various stations of life, have honoured them by their characteristic virtues. The object of the Church, in the selection of these saints, is, to convince us that salvation can be secured in all conditions of life, providing that the duties of them are fulfilled in a Christian manner.

We beseech Thee to admit us into the fellowship of the saints, *not in consideration of our merits, but of Thy own gratuitous pardon.* We ask of God to admit us among the number of His saints, not in consideration of our merits, but by granting us grace and showing us mercy; for if God should without mercy scrutinize our conduct, who could withstand His rigorous judgment? When

He grants life eternal, He grants it, not as a debt, but as a grace and a mercy. (Rom. vi. 23.)

We began this prayer by acknowledging that we were sinners. It is not upon our merits that we ground our hopes of mercy. We throw ourselves upon the multitude of God's tender mercies; we entreat Him to manifest them in all their extent, by granting blessings to which we have no right to pretend.

Since each of us has a particular patron in heaven, we beseech Him to listen to the prayers of His saints. That He would vouchsafe to accept this Sacrifice which they offer in union with us, and receive the blood of so many martyrs, united to the blood of His Son, as a host of propitiation. It is through Jesus Christ that we demand this favour. It is through Jesus Christ that we expect its fulfilment. It is through Jesus Christ that we hope to praise God throughout ages without end. Amen.

CONCLUSION OF THE CANON.

"All things were made by Him (Christ), and without Him was made nothing."—St. John i. 3.

It was in the name of Christ, that the priest just now solicited the admission into heaven of the living and of the dead. He now assigns the reason why he offered up all those petitions in the name of Jesus Christ, "it is because God grants all "favours and graces through Him, and that it is "through Him that God does always create, "sanctify, quicken, bless, and give us all these "good things." It is by Jesus Christ (by whom all things were made, St. John i.) that God *created* the bread and wine which are to become the matter of the Sacrifice. That He *sanctifies them*, choosing them to be the matter of the Sacrifice; *vivifies* them by substituting in their place Jesus Christ Himself, the living Bread descended from heaven; *blesses them*, because the Body and Blood of Christ produced by the change of the substance of bread and wine, are a sacrifice of adoration and praise offered to God, and a source of blessings to His church. And *He gives them* by the holy communion, in which we receive the true Body and Blood of Christ.

The signs of the cross, which are made during the pronouncing of those words, denote that the action, by which the bread and wine are sanctified and vivified, and become, by the change of substance, a source of graces and blessings, *is a representation and continuation of the Sacrifice of the Cross.*

In the above, you beheld a summary of what Christ has done in our behalf; let us now attend to the explanation of what the Church does *in* and *through* Him for the glory of His eternal Father.

" It is by Him, and with Him, and in Him,
" that all honour and glory are given to Thee,
" O God the Father Almighty, in the unity of
" the Holy Ghost, for ever and ever."

These words mean that the Sacrifice of Jesus Christ can alone render to God the honour that is due to Him; and that we cannot honour God worthily but *by* Jesus Christ, *with* Jesus Christ, and *in* Jesus Christ. *By Jesus Christ*, because He is the only Mediator, by whom we can please God. *With Jesus Christ*, because, in order to please God, and to render to Him the honour due to Him, we must be united to Christ in spirit, be animated with His dispositions, and depend on Him in all we do. *In Jesus Christ*, because we cannot please God unless we are as it were engrafted on Christ, as a branch is on the tree that bears it. The signs of the cross accompany these words, *by Him, &c.*, and signify that God can be honoured only by the Sacrifice of the Cross. The signs of the cross made on the altar, and accompanying these words, *"To Thee, Almighty God, the Father, in the unity of the Holy Ghost, all honour and "glory belong,"* mean, that it is by the cross, of which the altar is a figure or emblem, that the Holy Trinity which is here named, receives all honour and glory.

ON THE DEVOTION WITH WHICH WE SHOULD ASSIST AT THE HOLY SACRIFICE.

"Reverence My sanctuary; I am the Lord."—Leviticus xix. 30.
"He beheld the Invisible as if He were visible."—Heb. xi. 27.

Our principal devotion, from the moment of the Consecration till after the Communion, should be, a lively faith, a most profound reverence, and a heart inflamed for that Lamb of God who there offers Himself in sacrifice for us.

If, when God appeared to Moses in the burning bush in the desert, the place became holy in consequence of the Divine Presence, insomuch that God commanded him to take off his shoes, how much more holy does the place of our altars become, where Christ is present, as both our Priest and Victim.

When, at the dedication of the temple of Solomon, the priests had, with the greatest solemnity, placed the Ark of the Covenant in the Holy of Holies, a cloud filled the House of the Lord, so that they could no longer stand there to minister, the Glory of the Lord having filled the whole House. Yet this was but the shadow of the Divine Presence, whereas, on our altars, we have the reality thereof, veiled indeed from the eyes of our bodies, but visible to the eyes of our faith. "If, then, the "ministration of condemnation were glorious, "how much more does the ministration of glory "abound in glory, by reason of the glory that ex-"celleth."—(2 Cor. iii. 9.)

"While the sacrifice is being offered up," says St. Chrysostom, on the Priesthood, "the angels "stand by the priest; and the sanctuary is filled "with those heavenly spirits, robed in white, and "standing, with the utmost respect and reverence "towards the adorable Victim lying on the altar. "When you behold the priest at the altar making "the offering, do not think of the man, but con- "sider the hand of the Lord, which is invisibly "extended !.........When, again, you behold the "Lord of Glory, lying slain on the altar, the "priest praying over Him, and the multitude "surrounding the altar sprinkled with His Blood, "do you still consider yourselves on earth ? do you "not rather imagine yourselves delivered from the "shackles of the body, raised up to the heavens, "and, with the eyes of the naked soul, contem- "plating the things that are above ?" (S. Chrysostom, idem.)

With what profound respect did the people of God, in ancient times, reverence the sanctuary in which the Ark of the Covenant was placed ! How much more profoundly ought we to reverence the true sanctuary of God, and the Lord Himself of the covenant, who is present in our tremendous mysteries!

Our Saviour, in the Mass, officiates in person, and acts, as in a sacred tragedy, His whole Passion and death: we ought, then, to accompany Him therein with suitable affection and devotion. Had we, with true belief in Him, been present at the Sacrifice of the Cross, the Sacrifice of our Redemption, with what sentiments of love and gratitude, with what sorrow and repentance for our sins, with what fervour and devotion should we have waited upon Him, there reflecting on the heinous enormity of our sins, which could not be expiated but by His sacred Blood! With the like sentiments ought we to assist at this solemn memorial and representation of His Passion and Death.

"Faisons donc paroître par la retenue de nos
"sens, par la posture de notre corps, et par tout
"notre exterieur, une humilité profonde, une
"crainte religieuse et une vive foi de la presence
"de Jesus Christ, sur nos autels! Disons la sainte
"Messe avec un air de recueillment qui fasse
"connoître à ceux qui l'entêndent combien nous
"sommes convaincus et combien ils le doivent
"être, que Jesus Christ y est réellement présent
"accompagné d'une multitude d'anges qui l'ado-
"rent." (Tronson.)

THE REAL PRESENCE OF JESUS CHRIST IN THE EUCHARISTIC SACRIFICE AND SACRAMENT, PROVED FROM THE TESTIMONY OF THE HOLY FATHERS OF THE PRIMITIVE AGES OF CHRISTIANITY.

"This," said Christ, "is My Body. This is My " Blood."—St. Matthew xxvi. 26. 28.

In order to lay the foundations of His Church, the Son of God chose His apostles from the lowest grade of society, lest that their future success in establishing it might be attributed to their great mental abilities and eloquence, or to the influence of birth, education, and of riches, instead of to the efficacy of the Spirit of God, and to the merits of Christ's Passion and Death. But when the victory of Christianity over Paganism was won, the Spirit of God raised up a galaxy or phalanx of illustrious personages, endowed with all the gifts of nature and of grace, and animated with the Spirit of God, in order to complete the edifice of which the apostles had but laid the foundation, to level every height that might exalt itself against the knowledge of God, and to bring into captivity every understanding to the obedience of Christ.

These great personages became, through the Providence of God, the bishops of all the great cities of the then civilised world, which were the capitals of so many great kingdoms previously to their being absorbed by the Roman Empire: as Rome itself, Alexandria, Antioch, Constantinople, Jerusalem, Milan, Lyons, Carthage, Hippo, Cæsarea, Nazianzum, and other such cities. They were like so many beacons placed on the summits of high mountains, to enlighten by their writings the whole world until the end of time.

The fourth and fifth centuries of Christianity resemble the prophetic era inasmuch as God then raised up extraordinary personages endowed with supernatural gifts to accomplish His views and designs of mercy on mankind. The holy fathers are to the new law, what the prophets were to the old law. They are, by prescription, the Fathers of Christianity. These illustrious personages are unanimous witnesses, that the faith of the Real Presence of Christ in the Eucharistic Sacrifice and Sacrament was everywhere believed by all, and at all times; in other words, that it is universal as to time and place.

This alone proves the Divine and apostolical origin of that doctrine. For, since during the fourth and fifth centuries of Christianity it was universal; and as no trace of its origin posterior to the teaching of the apostles can be assigned, it is necessarily Divine.

Moreover, Protestants admit that no error, at

least of any moment, had crept into the Church previously to the fourth and fifth centuries of Christianity.

Let us now listen to a few of the testimonies of those great doctors on the existence of the faith of the Eucharistic Sacrifice and Sacrament in their respective times.

"We read," says St. Ambrose, "that, God "having spoken, all things were instantly made, "and, having commanded, all things were created. "If, then, the word of Christ, 'by Whom all "things were made, and without Whom nothing "of what was made, was made,' imparted exist- "ence to what had it not, can He not change the "nature of what already exists, since it is easier "to change the nature of what exists, than to "create?"—(Discourse to Neophytes, c. 9.)

St. Chrysostom, (forty-sixth Homily, on St. John's Gospel,) observes that "As those words, "*increase*, multiply, and *fill the earth*, having been "but once pronounced by God at the creation, still "continue to impart to human nature the power "of perpetuating itself by procreation until the "end of all time, so, in like manner, although the "words of Christ, *This is My Body, This is My* "*Blood*, were but once pronounced by Him, still "they continue to impart to this Sacrifice all its "virtue and efficacy which it has on the altars of

"the Church, and which it will have unto the end
" of all time."

St. Ambrose, while instructing those whom he was about to admit to the holy Sacraments, speaks thus : " You will," said he to them, " say to me, " How can you assure us that it is the Body and " Blood of Christ that we are about to receive, " since we behold quite another thing ? This I " will prove to you. I can furnish you numerous " instances that what we receive at the altar is " not what it was formed by nature, but what it " is become by consecration; which consecration " or benediction is much more powerful than " nature, since it is able to change the nature " itself of things. Thus Moses threw on the " ground the rod which he held in his hand, and " it became a serpent. He then caught the ser- " pent by the tail, and it immediately became a " rod again." Upon which, St. Cyril of Alexandria says, to those who denied the possibility of the change of bread and wine into the Blood of Christ : "If you persist in asking me how this " miraculous change takes place, I will insist " upon hearing from you, how the rod of Moses " was *changed* into a serpent, and how the waters " of the river Nile were *changed* into blood."

" At the command of the same Moses," says again St. Ambrose, " water flowed from the " rock in behalf of the Jews : but for you Chris-

"tians, Blood flows from the side of Jesus
"Christ. If the word of Elias was able to bring
"down the fire of heaven, shall not the word
"of Jesus Christ be able to change the nature of
"created things?"

"While being carried up to heaven," says St.
Chrysostom, "Elias let his mantle fall on his
"disciple Eliseus, and thereby deprived himself
"of it. Whereas Christ, ascending up to heaven,
"left us His Body and Blood, but without depriv-
"ing Himself of them, for He carried them up
"thither with Him.

"The birth which Jesus Christ assumed from
"Mary, did not follow the ordinary course of
"nature. It is certain that the order of nature
"was not observed therein, did not contribute to
"it. It is manifestly contrary to the order of
"nature that a virgin should become a mother,
"she still remaining a pure virgin. Why, then,
"seek the order of nature in the reproduction of
"the Body of Christ in this sacrament, since it
"was contrarily to the order of nature that this
"same Son was born of a virgin?

"At the wedding of Cana in Galilee, our
"Saviour, by the sole act of His will, changed
"water into wine, and shall He not be believed
"when He declares that He has changed the wine
"into His Blood?" (St. Chrysostom.)

The same holy father continues: "When a

"person asks how a thing can be done, he gives
"to understand that he does not consider it pos-
"sible. If, then, you ask how the bread and
"wine are changed into the Body and Blood of
"Christ, why do you not also ask how the five
"loaves and the few fishes were so multiplied as
"to feed several thousand persons?"

St. Chrysostom again says: "If the blood of a
"lamb saved the Israelites in Egypt from the
"destroying angel, not because it was blood, but
"because it represented the Blood of the true
"Lamb of God, how much more will the real
"Blood of the true Lamb of God itself put to flight
"the evil spirits, when they behold it, not sprinkled
"on our doors, but shining in our mouths."

"The treachery of Judas inspires us with horror,
"then let us take care not to become guilty of the
"same crime by an unworthy communion."

St. Augustine, and the successor of St. Cyril of
Jerusalem, hold nearly the same language. "Re-
"ceive," says the former, "under the appearance
"of bread, that same flesh which was nailed to the
"cross on Mount Calvary. Drink out of the
"chalice that same Blood which flowed from the
"side of our Saviour, when pierced with the lance
"on the cross." The latter declares that "the
"contents of the chalice on the altar are the same
"Blood that issued from the side of Christ when
"pierced with the lance." (Sermon 83.)

Lastly, "let us not consider the Eucharist to "be what it appears to our sight, but what "the words of Christ declare it to be." (St. Augustine.) See Discussion Amicale, vol. ii. p. 8.

The belief then in the real presence of Christ in the Eucharistic sacrifice and sacrament, is an important item of the faith once delivered to the saints, which the Church has ever guarded as the apple of her eye.

We do not pretend Christ to be present in the Eucharist in the same mode of existence as while He was upon earth; such is not the Catholic belief. We believe Him to be present in the Eucharist, in a *real*, but still in a spiritual mode of existence, such as His Body was after His resurrection. According to St. Paul, there are two different modes of being proper to the human body: "This corruptible body must put on in-"corruption, and this mortal body must put on "immortality." (1 Cor. xv. 53.) "There is," says he, "a natural body, and a spiritual body." (Id. 44.) Bearing this in mind, all difficulties vanish at once. The eye, the taste, the touch, may tell us that it is mere bread and wine; but they represent only appearances. In order to learn what the substance really is, we must listen to the word of God, which says: "*This is My* "*Body. This is My Blood.*" Mary Magdalen saw a young man at the sepulchre. (St. Mark xvi.)

St. Matthew tells us that it was not a young man, but an angel. (St. Matt. xxviii.) The same may be said of our other senses. "Faith cometh by hearing, and hearing by the word of Christ." (Rom. x. 17.)

FOURTH ARTICLE.

THE COMMUNION; OR FOURTH AND LAST PART OF THE LITURGY.

"The chalice of benediction which we bless, is it not "the communion of the Blood of Christ? And the "bread which we break, is it not the partaking of the "Body of the Lord?"—1 Cor. x. 16.

By means of the various prayers and ceremonies that accompany the different parts of the august Sacrifice of our altars, the Church has successively conducted us from the penitential to the instructive part; from the instructive part to the oblation; from the oblation to the consecration; and from the consecration to the communion, which is the third and last essential part of the Sacrifice.

We are not to confound *communion*, inasmuch as it is one of the essential parts of the Sacrifice of the Mass, with *communion*, as it is the fourth part of the liturgy. All the prayers of that part of the liturgy called *the communion*, which precede the consumption of the Sacred Elements, are an immediate preparation to it; and all the prayers that follow, to the end of the service, are a thanksgiving for it.

The Communion, or participation of the matter of the Sacrifice, is an essential part thereof. We have already had the oblation and Consecration, which correspond to the offering up and immolation of the Victim. The Communion is the consummation of the Sacrifice. The effects of the Sacrifice are, to some extent, suspended till the Communion is effected. So essential was the participation of the flesh of the victim considered under the old law, that in the holocausts, which were the most perfect kind of sacrifices, and in which the victim was totally burnt, in acknowledgment of God's supreme dominion over all things, a cake was at the same time offered up and eaten, that this essential part of sacrifice might not be wanting. In the Sacrifice of the New Law, which includes the perfection of former sacrifices, there is a similar consummation. So convinced is the Church of the necessity of Communion as an essential part of the Sacrifice of the Mass, that, should the minister, while engaged in this awful function, be surprised by some unforeseen accident, and rendered incapable of consummating the Sacrifice, she requires another minister to take his place, to consummate the Sacrifice, even though no one could be found that had not broken his fast. The Communion concludes the

Sacrifice, makes it perfect in all its parts, and leaves nothing more to be desired.

In accordance with this doctrine of the Church is that of St. Paul in the above text, (1 Cor. x. 16.) "The chalice of benediction which we bless, is it "not the communion of the Blood of Christ? "And the bread which we break, is it not the "participation of the Body of the Lord?" The apostle does not here separate the blessing of the cup, and the breaking of the bread, from the communion of the Blood, and the participation of the Body, of Christ. In other words, he considers the communion essentially and inseparably connected with the consecration, and as part and parcel of the Sacrifice.

PREPARATION FOR THE SACRIFICIAL COMMUNION.

The prayers for this purpose are, the Lord's Prayer, the two short prayers *Pax Domini* and *Hæc commixtio, &c.*, the *Agnus Dei*, the three following prayers, and the *Domine non sum dignus*.

THE LORD'S PRAYER.

"Teach us to pray."—St. Luke xi. 1.

Prayer is the most infallible means to obtain all good from God, when it flows from an humble heart, wholly relying on His mercy, and on the merits of Christ, and offered up in His name, and in union with Him.

The Lord's Prayer is the most excellent of all prayers. It was composed, not by a saint, nor by a prophet, nor even by an angel, or archangel, but by our Lord Jesus Christ Himself, the Son and Eternal Wisdom of God. And where or when can it be so intimately united with Christ, or so effectually offered up in His name, as when joined with the adorable Sacrifice of His Blessed Body and Blood, and offered up in union with those divine mysteries? It contains every perfect form of adoration; it is a summary of all the truths of salvation, of all the demands that a Christian can make for the glory of God, for his own salvation, for that of his neighbour, and for every succour, both spiritual and temporal, of which he may stand in need. It likewise contains an abridgment of the dispositions which should accompany us to the foot of the altar. We may add that whoever has repeated it with a lively faith and undeviating attention, cannot possibly have anything further to demand of God.

The faithful conclude this prayer with the words, *Deliver us from evil.* Deliver us from evil, that Thou, O God, mayest be glorified in us; that Thou mayest reign over us; that we may do Thy will; that we may obtain of Thy bounty all spiritual and temporal advantages; that we may deserve the pardon of our sins on account of our sincere love of our brethren; and that our weakness may not be exposed to temptations.

The priest answers *Amen, so be it,* may you be delivered from all evil.

He then explains this desire of the faithful of being delivered from evil, by mentioning the evils from which they desire deliverance, and the names of those through whose mediation they expect it. "Deliver us," says he, "from all "evils, past, present, and to come, and through "the intercession of the glorious Mary, ever a "Virgin, of the Blessed Apostles, Peter, Paul, "and Andrew, and of all the saints, grant us, as "the effect of Thy mercy, peace in our days, that, "being supported by the help of Thy mercy, we "may be delivered from all sin, and exempted "from every kind of trouble, through Christ our "Lord."

Present and past evils here mean our manifold sins; and the evils to come mean the just chastisement of our offences, which would follow, if our prayers, and those more powerful ones of the saints, who intercede for us, intercepted not the justice, or excited not the mercy of God.

Taking hold of the paten at the words of the above prayer, *grant us peace*, the priest therewith makes on himself the sign of the cross, because it is by means of the cross that all opposition to our peace is removed.

THE PAX DOMINI AND THE PRAYER HÆC COMMIXTIO, TOGETHER WITH THE ACCOMPANYING CEREMONY.

"Christ, rising from the dead, dieth now no more."
—Rom. vi. 9.

The resurrection of Jesus Christ is the most consoling truth of religion. It proves that our faith is not vain, nor our hopes insecure or groundless; for since, after having undergone the punishment of sin, He is risen, He had only the appearance of guilt; its stain did not reach His soul, He is not less true in His words than admirable in His miracles and works.

Immediately after the Lord's Prayer, the priest takes in his hands the Sacred Host, raises It above the chalice, and breaks It into two equal parts, one of which he places upon the altar: detaching a particle from the other half, and making with it the sign of the cross three times over the chalice, he says: "*May the peace of the Lord be ever with you.*" He then drops the particle into the chalice, saying: "*May this mixture of the Body and Blood of our Lord Jesus Christ become to us, who are about to receive it, a pledge of eternal life.*"

The Sacrifice of the Mass being a continuation of the Sacrifice of the Cross, and the ceremonies of the Mass being an actual representation of the circumstances of the Sacrifice of the Cross, the principal circumstances of the Sacrifice of the Cross should therefore be pointed out by corresponding ceremonies in the Mass. Now, there are two principal circumstances in the Sacrifice of our Redemption,—Christ's Death and Resurrection. The Death and Resurrection of Christ are the two principal mysteries of the Christian religion. His Death is the proof of His humanity, while His Resurrection confirms the truth of His Divinity, and consequently His dominion over life and death. His death was the effect of His conflict with the powers of darkness; His Resurrection the signal of His victory over them. And as the Church in the Mass represents Christ's Death by the words of consecration, saying, "*This is My Body: This is My Blood which shall be shed for you*,"—so, when the two species are united in the chalice, their union represents the reunion of Christ's Soul and Body, which took place at the moment of His Resurrection. The action of the priest in letting the particle of the Sacred Host fall into the chalice, is representative of the moment when the supreme Deliverer raised Himself from the tomb, and rendered us for ever secure of the fruits of His Passion. The Body and Blood of Christ, which are represented as separated at the moment of the consecration by the sacrificial words, are here represented as reunited by the mixture of the two sacred species, accompanied by the words, "*May this mixture* "*and consecration of Christ's Body and Blood be* "*effectual unto eternal life to us who receive it.*"

The temple of Christ's Body is represented as destroyed and re-established, by the two-fold representation of the mysteries of Christ's Death and Resurrection, upon our altars: the Sacrifice of the Mass is accordingly offered up, not only in memory of Christ's Passion and Death, but also of His Resurrection and Ascension. It is therefore absolutely necessary that in some part of the Mass the reunion of Christ's Soul and Body should be represented, that it may be announced that Christ *ever liveth to make intercession for us.* The breaking of the Sacred Host reminds us of one of the most venerable recollections of religion; for, taking the bread, He broke it and gave it to His disciples, saying: "*Take ye, and eat of* "*this.*" (St. Matt. xxvi.)

The priest makes three signs of the cross with the particle over the chalice, before letting it fall into it, saying : "*May the peace of the Lord be always with you.*"

Peace be to you, is the salutation with which Christ always greeted His Apostles after His Resurrection, as the fruits of His Death and Resurrection, He having been "*delivered for our sins, and risen for our justification.*" But what kind of peace is this that the priest wishes to the faithful ? It is, first, the peace of God, the sole inheritance which Christ, from the summit of the cross, bequeathed to His followers. Secondly, The peace of conscience, which the world cannot give, and which is the fruit of our victory over our passions. The former of these is a necessary disposition for Holy Communion; the latter is the effect of a worthy Communion.

In ancient times alliances were contracted by sealing them with the blood of the victims then offered up in sacrifice, or by the blood of the contracting parties themselves, which each drew from his own veins. It is not with the blood of animals, nor even with mere human blood, but with the Blood of the God-Man, that the peace and union of all Christians between themselves and with God, is here sealed. It is a perpetual and universal peace that the Church asks by this prayer : "*May the peace of the Lord be always with you,*" as the fruit of the sacrifice of Jesus Christ, which is offered up by the consecration, and consummated by the communion.

"For it is by this divine Blood that all things "have been pacified, and heaven and earth recon-"ciled, Christ making peace through the Blood of "His Cross, both as to the things that are on "earth, and to the things that are in heaven." (Col. i. 20.) And lastly, it is in honour of the Holy Trinity that the three signs of the cross are made. The faithful should, at this moment, make an act of the love of their neighbours in conformity with the above short prayer, "May the peace of the Lord be always with you."

THE AGNUS DEI.

"Behold the Lamb of God, who taketh away the sins "of the world."—St. John i. 29.

The union of the two species in the chalice represents the union of the Divine and human natures, which took place at the Incarnation, the union of God and man that takes place in the Holy Communion, and the union which will take place when all the saints of God are united in heaven in peace and unity. But how are these desirable unions obtained unless we have a victim which can make satisfaction for our sins, and reconcile us to God; for, while there exists between God and us a wall of separation which has been raised up by our sins, no union between God and us is possible. Aware of this, the Church addresses herself to Jesus Christ, as the *Lamb* and *Victim of God*, to take away our sins.

The Messiah is frequently designated by the prophets as a *lamb*, in reference to His becoming on the Cross a Victim for the sins of the world. Thus, in the Apocalypse, He is styled, "*the Lamb* "*slain from the beginning of the world.*" (Apoc. xiii. 8.) The Prophet Isaias prayed for His coming under this title: "Send forth, O Lord, "the Lamb, the ruler of the earth, to the mount " of the daughter of Sion." (xvi. 1.) The same prophet foretells His unalterable patience and mildness during His Passion, by representing Him as a sheep that is led to the slaughter, and as a lamb before the shearer, that does not open His mouth. In accordance with these prophecies, the Baptist points Him out to the multitude, as the frequently foretold and long expected Lamb, that was to take away the sins of the world. Hence, while Jesus Christ is being offered up a Victim on our altars, the Church addresses Him thus: "*Lamb of God, who takest away the* "*sins of the world.*" She invokes Him in this manner three times, a practice which she always observes in the case of those formularies which appear to her of more than ordinary importance, and to show the great need we have of God's mercy and grace, in order to be reconciled to Him in this life, and to be united to Him in the next. The priest pronounces these words in a bending posture, to denote the sentiments of awe and veneration which they should excite in every heart. He strikes his breast three times at the words, "*Have mercy on us*," because he regards his sins as the most proper motive to excite the tender compassion of Jesus Christ. At the third repetition, he changes the object by soliciting peace because the compassion of Christ is particularly directed to the trouble produced within us by sin.

Yes, the Victim which the Church presents in the Sacrifice of the Mass is truly the Sacrifice of God, the Oblation of God, the *Lamb of God*, chosen by a God, offered by a God, accepted by a God, alone worthy of a God, alone capable of appeasing a God, and of effecting a reconciliation between God and His offending creatures.

"*Who takest away the sins of the world.*"— God laid upon His shoulders the iniquities of us all; He bears on them the sins of the whole world; He is loaded with our sorrows; He is covered with our bruises; and, without contracting the pollution of sin, He becomes, in some measure, sin itself, that He may blot out our transgressions. *He became sin for us.*—That is, the representative of sin, who was to bear the whole weight of the Divine indignation; the pledge for sin, by making an infinite reparation to the offended majesty of God. The *remedy for sin*, the wounds of which were too deep for aught but the merits of a God to cure; there was not a single transgression committed from the beginning of the world, for which He did not make ample satisfaction to His Eternal Father.

Encouraged by those considerations, let us not yield to dejection or despair; and whilst the Church, in the name of all her children, exclaims, "Have mercy on us," penetrated with grief at the sight of our infidelities, we too should repeat with fervour, " O Lord, Thou knowest the dust " out of which we are formed; Thou knowest the " weakness of our nature, since Thou hast felt "the bitter effects of our sins, in the pangs of " Thy Passion and Death. *Have mercy on us:* " show us compassion; we are the sheep of Thy "fold; save us from the rage of the wolves that " are continually prowling around the fold to sur- "prise and devour us. *Have mercy on us* for the " glory of Thy name; ensure to us the fruits of " Thy Passion; let not Thy blood be shed for us " in vain. *Grant us Thy peace:* O Divine Lamb, " who didst come to bring peace upon earth, " to effect our peace with heaven, grant us Thy "peace in both time and eternity."

Could there be a more appropriate preparatory prayer for Communion? The first and most essential preparation for Communion is the absence at least of mortal sin, and who but Christ can deliver us from sin, the great obstacle to our union with God in time and eternity?

THREE PRAYERS IN IMMEDIATE PREPARATION FOR THE COMMUNION OF THE PRIEST.

THE FIRST PRAYER.

"Before all things have a constant mutual charity; "for charity covereth a multitude of sins."—1 St. Peter iv. 8.

The Holy Eucharist is the sacrament of love and of peace; Christ is the Prince of Peace; heaven the abode of peace. None but those who have been men of peace in this life, will ever make fit subjects for enjoying the harmony of heaven. The apostle exhorts us to endeavour to be at peace with all men; without which no one will ever see God. And Christ enjoins us this, saying: "If "thou bring thy gift to the altar, and there re- "member that thy brother has aught against thee, "leave there thy gift before the altar; go first to "be reconciled to thy brother, and then come and "offer thy gift." (St. Matt. v.—Discourse on the Mount.) Moreover, in order to become, by means of the Holy Communion, one body and one spirit with Christ, we must be so united among ourselves by mutual charity as to form but one heart and one soul. So essential is this disposition to a worthy communion, that the Church asks it of God with increased fervour in the following prayer: "O "Lord Jesus Christ, who didst say to Thine apos- "tles, Peace I leave you, My peace I give you, "regard not my sins, but the faith of Thy "Church; and vouchsafe, according to Thy will, "to pacify and unite it."

In Masses for the dead this prayer is omitted, for the peace which we solicit for the Church Militant, is not suitable to the condition of the Church Suffering in purgatory, but is most necessary for ourselves, who are living in the midst of trials, temptations and dangers; and lest that our sins should render us unworthy of obtaining it, the priest asks it through the faith of the Church; faith alone prays, and the Church, being the sole abode of faith, is also the sole house of prayer. The Catholic Church, to the exclusion of all sects, has alone received the gift of prayer.

THE SECOND PRAYER.

"Who shall separate us from the love of Christ?"—Romans viii. 35.

The second prayer is as follows: "O Lord Jesus "Christ, Son of the Living God, who, by the will "of the Eternal Father, and with the cooperation of "the Holy Ghost, hast by Thy Death given life to "the world, deliver me, by Thy most sacred Body "and Blood, from all my iniquities, and from all "evils, and make me always adhere to Thy com- "mandments, and never permit me to be sepa- "rated from Thee, who, with the Father and the " Holy Ghost, livest and reignest, God world "without end. Amen."

This prayer reminds us that it was the Death of Christ that gave life to the world; we partake of the benefits of Christ's Death by the Holy Communion, as the Jews of old partook of the benefits of the legal sacrifices, by partaking of the flesh of the victims; they thus communed with God by means of the sacrifices offered up to Him. In like manner, the Eucharistic participation of the Body and Blood of Christ was instituted as a means of invisibly and interiorly communicating to us the grace and spirit of all the mysteries of the God-Man.

This prayer contains three most excellent requests.—1. To be freed from all iniquities; because innocence is the first and most essential disposition for communion. 2. That having obtained that innocence we may never lose it, but always remain steadfast in fulfilling all the commands of God. And 3rd. That when once we shall have had the happiness of being united to Christ we may never more be separated from Him. "May "I, O Lord, in this world always live to Thee, be "guided by Thy Spirit; and in the next life not "be doomed to that greatest punishment of Thy "enemies, which consists in an eternal separation "from Thee."

THE THIRD PRAYER.

" He that eats and drinks unworthily, eats and drinks "judgment to himself."—1 Cor. xi. 29.

This prayer is deprecatory of evils and supplicatory of benefits. The priest, inspired by the sense of his own unworthiness, prays thus : " Let "not, O Lord Jesus Christ, the participation of "Thy Body, which I unworthily presume to receive, "be to me unto judgment and condemnation, but "according to Thy goodness, let it profit me to "the safe keeping of soul and body, and to spiri- "tual healing."

The priest here renews his sentiments of humility and compunction, and entreats our Lord that His adorable Body may prove a preservative against mortal sins, and a salutary remedy of venial sins.

DOMINE NON SUM DIGNUS.

"Lord, I am not worthy that Thou shouldst enter "under my roof: say but the word, and my servant "shall be healed.—St. Matt. viii. 8.

The preceding prayers being ended, the priest kneels to adore our Lord, whom he is about to receive. St. Augustine says: "No one doth eat "the Flesh of Christ till he has first adored "Him." Then, rising and taking the Sacred Host in his hands, he says, "I will take the "heavenly Bread, and I will call upon the name "of the Lord." Immediately afterwards, holding the Sacred Host in his left hand, and looking at it with awe and affection, with the right hand he three times strikes his breast, repeating each time: "*Lord, I am not worthy that Thou* "*shouldst enter under my roof: say but the word,* "*and my soul shall be healed.*" (St. Matt. viii.) At each repetition, a bell is rung, to excite the attention of the faithful to this part of the Mass, which exceeds in importance every other part, except the consecration. Those words, "*Lord, I* "*am not worthy,*" &c., are, at the same time a most profound acknowledgment of his own unworthiness, and an act of his lively faith in the divinity and goodness of Jesus Christ. They were first uttered by a Roman centurion to our Saviour, who answered him that He would go down to his house to restore his servant to health. "No, Lord," replied he, "I am not worthy of "so great an honour; say but the word where "Thou art standing, and my servant will be "instantly healed." With great propriety and singular beauty has the Church adapted these words to the present subject. Our Lord is about to enter into our breasts, and we in astonishment exclaim: "No, Lord, our breasts are not fit "abodes for Thee: what is there in us but sin, "guilt, and defilement? If Thou, O Lord, must "come, be first our Physician, and heal our souls "of their infirmities. Speak the word, and the "thing shall be done. Who shall presume to "present himself at Thy table? Shall we dare "to receive Thee after having defiled the white "robes of innocence with which we were clothed "in baptism? Shall we present ourselves at "Thy feast without the nuptial garment of inno- "cence? Where are our tears, our repentance, "our sorrow? Shall we then give ourselves up "to despair at the sight of our miseries? Where "shall we go to seek that support of which we "stand so much in need? We will rather hasten

"to comply with that tender invitation which we
"have already heard from Thy divine lips:
"Come to Me all ye that labour and are heavily
"laden, and I will refresh you, and you shall find
"rest to your souls. Yes, Lord, we will go to
"Thee, for we know that if Thou sayest but one
"word, our souls will be instantly healed. A
"single word of Thine is sufficient to perform the
"greatest prodigies of love. *Say but the word,
"and my soul shall be healed.*"

THE COMMUNION OF THE PRIEST.

"I will take the chalice of salvation, and will call
"upon the name of the Lord."—Psalm cxv.

To the triple confession of his unworthiness, the priest adds this short prayer: "May the "Body of our Lord Jesus Christ preserve my "soul unto everlasting life. Amen." Then, making with the Sacred Host the sign of the cross, he immediately receives it into his breast. Uncovering afterwards the chalice, he kneels to adore the Sacred Blood also. Rising up, he says: "What "return shall I make to the Lord for all He has "given me? I will call upon the Lord in praise, "and I shall be free from my enemies." Then, taking the chalice into his hands, and making with it the sign of the cross, as he previously did with the Host, he says: "May the Blood of our Lord Jesus Christ preserve my soul unto everlasting life," and immediately receives it.

He then distributes the Blessed Sacrament to the laity, if there be any prepared to receive it.

And thus are finished all the essential parts of the Sacrifice. The Victim has disappeared from the altar; the Sacrifice is accomplished. The wine and water which are subsequently poured into the chalice are merely for the purpose of consuming any remains of the sacramental species that might remain in the chalice, and are therefore called *purifications*.

It is worthy of observation that all the prayers, from the *Agnus Dei*, inclusively to the Post Communion, are addressed to Jesus Christ, because all those prayers relate directly to the act of Holy Communion.

COMMUNION OF THE FAITHFUL NO ESSENTIAL PART OF THE SACRIFICE.

We have seen above that the communion of the priest is an essential part of the august Sacrifice of our altars; it is, of all the parts thereof, the most interesting, since it is thereby that the fruits of the Sacrifice are communicated to our souls. But we are not to conclude that the participation of the Victim by the faithful, who encompass the altar, is of equal necessity in order to the existence of the Sacrifice; for the actual practice of the Church detracts from this necessity. The communion of the faithful is indeed an integral part of the Sacrifice, but not an essential one. The Sacrifice, though deficient in one of its integral parts, still exists without it.

THE COMMUNION OF THE FAITHFUL A DIVINE PRECEPT.

Our Saviour says: "Except you eat the flesh "of the Son of Man, and drink His Blood, you "shall not have life in you. He that eateth My "Flesh and drinketh My Blood hath everlasting "life, and I will raise Him up at the last day. "For My Flesh is meat indeed, and My Blood is "drink indeed. He that eateth My Flesh and "drinketh My Blood, abideth in Me, and I in "him. As the Living Father hath sent Me, and "I live by the Father, so he that eateth Me, the "same shall live by Me." (St. John vi. 54, &c.)

The Church, in the Fourth Council of Lateran, declared the divine precept of receiving the Holy Communion to be obligatory on all persons that are come to the age of reason, *at least once in the year;* and it has fixed the time for receiving it about Easter, in memory of the great Paschal solemnity.

The Council of Trent, while wishing to revive frequent Communion, which had fallen into disuse among the laity, does not indeed prescribe it, but *entreats* the faithful to be moved by the consideration that it is the most holy action they can perform; it being a preservative against mortal sin, a remedy for venial sin, and the seed of immortality, preserving souls to life eternal. It is the desire of the Council that, as in former times, so now, a priest may never have occasion to offer up the Holy Sacrifice without having at least some of his flock prepared to join with him in Holy Communion.

DAILY COMMUNION IN THE PRIMITIVE CHURCH.

In the primitive Church, until the sixth century, all present at the Holy Sacrifice received the Holy Communion; there was then, for receiving it, no difference between days more or less solemn. Every day that beheld the first Christian in the place of worship, was to him in that respect an important festival; for all were then thoroughly instructed in their religion; they were sensible of the benefits of Holy Communion and appreciated its excellence. Their faith was vigorous and lively; they were full of the fear of God, and anxious to observe His commandments; their fervour was glowing and their charity ardent; they had a hunger and thirst after justice, and a strong desire of the salvation of their souls. How lovely were then thy tabernacles, O Jacob, and thy tents, O Israel! May my soul die the death of the just, and may my end be like unto theirs! (Numbers xxiv.)

As the communion of a whole congregation took up a considerable time, appropriate psalms or canticles were sung in the interval. The banquets of kings and of the great ones of the earth are always accompanied with singing and music; in like manner, the Christian temples resounded with melodious accents during this sacred feast, to which God, as the Host, the Food, and the Guest, invited His children; and while the sacred edifices resounded with canticles of divine praise, the angels who were present repeated on their golden harps the goodness of God and the happiness of man.

In the Eastern churches, it was the forty-first Psalm that was ordinarily sung. "As the hart "panteth after the fountains of water, so my soul "panteth after Thee, O my God! My soul hath "thirsted after the strong and living God. When "shall I come and appear before the face of my "God? My tears have been my bread day and "night, whilst it was said to me, Where is thy "God? With me is prayer to Thee the God of "my heart. I will say to my God, Thou art my "support. Hope thou in God, for I will give "praise to Him, the salvation of my countenance "and my God."

In the Western churches, it was the thirty-third Psalm that was sung on the same occasion. "I will bless the Lord at all times; His praise "shall be ever in my mouth. O magnify the "Lord with me, and let us extol His name "together. Come ye to Him and be enlightened. "The angel of the Lord shall encamp round "about those that fear Him, and shall deliver "them. O taste and see that the Lord is sweet; "blessed is the man that hopeth in Him. Fear "the Lord all ye saints; for there is no want to "them that fear Him. Turn away from evil, and "do good; seek after peace and pursue it."

SPIRITUAL COMMUNION.

"My words are spirit and life."—St. John vi. 64.

If the greater number cannot be persuaded to partake of the daily Victim, let them not turn away altogether empty from the sacred table. They may still derive an immense advantage, although they do not actually partake of it. This is done by spiritual communion.

Spiritual communion consists in an ardent desire to be spiritually united to Jesus Christ, since circumstances prevent for awhile a real union. It includes a desire of sacramental communion. The following is a specimen of spiritual communion. "My Jesus, I believe Thou art "present in the most holy Sacrament. I love "Thee above all things; I desire to receive Thee "into my soul. Since I cannot now receive Thee "sacramentally, come at least spiritually into my "heart. I embrace Thee, and unite myself en-"tirely to Thee, as if I had actually received "Thee. Never permit me to be separated from "Thee."

No one can be said to have assisted at Mass, according to the spirit of the Church, unless he has united himself, by at least a spiritual communion, to the adorable Victim offered up on our altars.

The Council of Trent extols the advantages of spiritual communion, and exhorts the faithful to avail themselves of it. This Council distinguishes three kinds of communion, a solely sacramental one, one that is both sacramental and spiritual, and one that is spiritual only. "Those," says the Council, "communicate spiritually, who with a "lively faith, which worketh by charity, desire to "partake of the holy Communion; such derive "great benefits therefrom."

DISPOSITIONS FOR A SPIRITUAL COMMUNION.

As one would derive no benefit from receiving Holy Communion in the state of mortal sin, so no benefit can be derived from a spiritual communion as long as one's affections are fixed on sin. To wish to be united to the God of all purity while in that state, would be to provoke His indignation. In order to a worthy spiritual communion, all causes of enmity between God and the sinner must be first removed. This is done by a sincere repentance and a resolution of expelling from one's soul all sinful affections, which render it an unfit abode for Jesus Christ. Hence, sinners, who will not take the pains to obtain contrition for their sins, and to correct their vices, cannot be united to Jesus Christ, even by a spiritual communion. Our Blessed Saviour indeed invites all who are heavily laden to come to Him, but no one can derive a benefit from approaching Him who does not first seek to be eased of his burden. Still, the absence of sin or of vice is but a negative disposition for spiritual communion. The soul that aspires to an union with its Saviour must be adorned with virtues; hence, acts of several virtues must be made at this part of the Mass, namely:

1. An act of faith in the real presence of Jesus Christ in the Eucharist. We must believe the positive declaration of God in preference to the remonstrances of our own weak and blind reason.

2. Of hope, founded on the promises which Jesus Christ has annexed to a worthy participation of Himself.

3. An act of desire to be united to the source of every blessing.

4. An act of humility; for God, who rejects the proud, always looks with complacency on the humble.

Spiritual communion greatly nourishes piety, keeps alive the flame of virtue, imparts sanctity to every affection, and increases the gifts of grace, by habituating our souls to a continual union with God at present, and by preparing them for an eternal union with Him in heaven.

THANKSGIVING AFTER COMMUNION.

"Give thanks to God, the Father of our Lord Jesus "Christ, praying always."—Col. i. 3.

The remaining portion of the Liturgy is set apart by the Church as a marked and prominent testimony of our gratitude to God, through Jesus Christ, *for the inestimable mystery just operated on our altars, and for the multitude of graces thereby poured out upon His whole Church.* Gratitude is a duty strongly enjoined by religion; for our Saviour condemned the conduct of those who, after having been miraculously healed by Himself of leprosy, did not return to give Him thanks. "Were there not," said He, "ten made clean? And where are the nine? "There is no one found to return to give glory to "God but this stranger." But in the Mass God imparts to us the greatest of favours, and the Church is most punctual in returning Him due thanks for them.

She has invariably done so in all ages; hence St. Augustine says: "Having partaken of the "great sacrament, the service concludes with the "solemn thanksgiving." May our gratitude to God equal that of our forefathers in the faith, gratitude being a no less essential disposition to secure the fruits of the Eucharist than those above pointed out. Hence the last prayers of the Liturgy have an equal claim to our attention and fervour.

THE ANTHEM CALLED THE COMMUNION.

Since the decline of the primitive fervour of Christians, and the consequent diminution of the number of communicants, instead of a whole psalm being chanted at this time, as was then usual, a single verse is read by the priest at the epistle corner of the altar. At first it never varied, and was, "*Taste and see that the Lord is sweet.*"

The present practice of the Church is, to select from some psalm a single verse which is at once applicable to the mystery of the day, and to the particular graces imparted to those who communicate worthily. These verses always contain the strongest motives to excite us to a constant union with Jesus Christ in the sacrament of His Body and Blood.

The above anthem is followed by the ordinary salutation from the middle of the altar, of *Dominus vobiscum,* which has here a particular signification, as if he said: You have now gone through, with me, the different parts of the Mass; you have partaken of the Victim which I have been offering, either in reality or in spirit: I therefore wish that the Lord may always remain with you, and take up His abode in your souls by a permanent residence, according to His promise, "He that eats My Flesh and drinks My "Blood, abideth in Me and I in Him."

THE POST COMMUNION.

This prayer, which is read at the Epistle corner, is properly a prayer of thanksgiving. Every collect, whether of the season or occasional, has its proper *Secret* and *Post Communion*, it being proper that the number of thanksgivings be equal to that of the petitions. As the Post Communions correspond in number with the Collects, so they likewise do in subject, form, and ceremonies. The Collect asks for general blessings, without any special reference to the Sacrifice. The Secret adverts to the Sacrifice about to be offered up; and the Post Communion alludes to the fruits which the Communion should produce in our souls. The object of the Post Communion is to ratify the good effects which faith authorises us to expect from a worthy Communion, and, therefore, it always contains mention of the Blessed Sacrament.

After the Post Communion, the priest and people salute each other for the last time, with the usual benediction, *Dominus Vobiscum*, which here means, May the Lord be with you to enlighten you, protect you, console you, and preserve in your souls the fruits of the Holy Sacrifice at which you have just assisted, and may you always be mindful of what you have this day beheld and done.

The people, full of gratitude to the priest who has just offered up for them the great Sacrifice, answer, *And with thy spirit,*—that is, we wish you the same blessings and graces which you wish us.

ITE, MISSA EST—DEPART, THE DIVINE SERVICE IS NOW OVER.

Docile to the voice of their pastors, the faithful, in assembling in the holy place, had listened to the suggestions of their fervour only. But it has always been found necessary to give them the signal to withdraw, they being aware that whatever appertained to this holy exercise, partook of the sanctity of that Victim from whose saving merits all the foregoing prayers and ceremonies have derived the whole of their efficacy.

The congregation, through the clerk, answer: *Thanks be to God!* Yes, eternal, infinite thanks are due to God every time He confers on us the happiness of assisting at this most wholesome sacrifice! Thanks be to God for having left us this Victim! Thanks be to God for the opportunity afforded us of assisting at the immolation thereof, of which blessing, so many others, more deserving than ourselves, are deprived.

PLACEAT OBSEQUIUM, &c.

The priest now turns to the altar, and, reflecting on the great action he has just presumed to perform, bows down his head, and repeats, in the spirit of humility, this last prayer of the Mass, which is extremely suitable to the occasion: " May the obedience of my service be pleasing to " Thee, O Blessed Trinity; and may the sacrifice " which I, though unworthy, have offered in the " sight of Thy divine majesty, be acceptable to " Thee, and, through Thy mercy, be a propitia- " tion for me, and for all those for whom I have " offered it, through Jesus Christ our Lord." As if he said : The service I have been performing is so great that I never should have presumed to perform it, had it not been in obedience to the command of my Saviour, who has chosen so unworthy a creature as myself to perform so great a service. May His goodness supersede my unworthiness, and grant a blessing to me, and to all for whom the sacrifice has been offered.

LAST BLESSING.

"And Aaron, stretching forth his hand towards the "people, blessed them, and the sacrifices being finished, "he came down."—Levit. ix. 22.

One of the powers which a priest receives at his ordination is that of blessing both persons and things. In this, as in all his other public functions, he is but the instrument, the channel, through which the blessings of the Almighty flow, the representative of Christ. In imparting the benediction, which he is about to pronounce, he represents, in his person, the whole Church, of which he is a minister; it is in her name, and in the name of Christ, that he pronounces the words of grace and benediction, which he draws from the fountains of our Saviour. He first kisses the altar, which represents Jesus Christ, the Author of all graces; then, lifting up his hands towards heaven, whence all graces are derived, and turning towards the people, he makes over them the sign of the cross, which invariably accompanies every benediction, it being from the cross of Christ that every grace is derived. He invokes the Almighty, Father, Son, and Holy Ghost, saying, in effect:

"*May God the Father bless you, who in Jesus*

"*Christ has blessed us with all spiritual bless-*
"*ings, that we may become His spiritual children,*
"*for the praise and glory of His grace.*"

"*May God the Son bless you, in whom the*
"*Father has made us agreeable in His sight,*
"*and who has redeemed us with His Blood,*
"*granting us the remission of our sins, and in*
"*whom all things, in heaven and on earth, are*
"*united, as in their head and chief.*

"*May God the Holy Ghost bless you, Who*
"*is the spirit of wisdom and of revelation, by*
"*whom we know God, and the seal by which we*
"*have been sealed to believe in Jesus Christ.*"

Can we doubt the efficacy of this blessing, if, by our own indevotion and obstinacy in sin, we do not counteract its salutary effects ? Let me address you in the words of the Pontifical : " Bow
" down your heads to receive this benediction ; it
" is the blessing of Him, at whose word all
" things started into existence. His name is
" the only source, whence all blessings and graces
" flow. Humble yourselves under His mighty
" hand, since He imparts His graces to none but
" the humble, to those who place no dependance
" on themselves, but expect all things at His
" hand. May the Almighty God, who exerts
" His power only to manifest His mercy, bless
" this people, whom He has created for His glory,
" ransomed by His Blood, and sanctified by His

"Spirit. The faithful should, with all the sin-
"cerity of their hearts, answer *Amen* to this last
"blessing of the Mass; and let it be an *Amen*
"never to be contradicted by their actions, never
"to be belied by their infidelities, which dry
"up the bounteous source of benedictions and
"graces."

THE LAST GOSPEL.

"This is the disciple who wrote these things, and we
"know that his testimony is true."—St. John xxi. 24.

The faithful have, in all ages, had a particular respect for the Gospel of St. John, as the most sublime of all the Gospels, and especially for this introductory chapter, which is one of the loftiest passages of all the inspired writings, and contains an excellent profession of faith in the divinity and humanity of Jesus Christ. A heathen philosopher was so struck with admiration at this Gospel, that he declared it ought to be written in golden letters on the most prominent part of every church. The Church commands it to be daily read, that it may be engraven on the hearts of the faithful, and be more present to our inmost thoughts than the most brilliant letters could represent it to our eyes.

This Gospel is read with the same ceremonies as the Gospel at the commencement of the Mass.

At the words, "*And the Word was made Flesh,*" all kneel down to adore Him who condescended to become man for our sakes, and to conceal His glory under the vile form of a slave.

This Gospel is an abridgment of all that the Son of God has done for us in both time and eternity. St. John, before declaring to us the Incarnation of the Word, makes a full declaration of His Divinity, that we may have an idea of His humility in descending so low from such a height.

It shows Him in the bosom of His Eternal Father, God, equal to Him, and tells us that by Him all things were made, and He is the life and the light of the world.

It shows Him descended upon earth, the true Sun of Justice, that shone in the darkness of this world, and enlightened those that sat in the shadow of death. It reminds us that it was by Him that we were made the children of God; for He took upon Him our nature, and dwelt amongst us, to redeem us from the slavery of sin and to deliver us from eternal damnation.

We beheld His glory in the manger, on Mounts Thabor and Calvary, and at His tomb; we daily behold it in the Holy Eucharist; and we praise and bless Him because He is full of grace and truth.

The Word made Flesh has proved to us,—in

prayer, a powerful intercessor; in the Oblation, a Victim of salvation; and in the Communion, the Bread of Life. May He prove to us, amidst the various occupations of life, a model, a pastor, and a guide; that, as He dwells amongst us by His presence in the Eucharist, so we may merit, by His grace, to dwell with Him for all eternity.

The assembled multitude, by the mouth of the clerk, answer, *Deo gratias*—Thanks be to God. So short, so holy, so perfect, so worthy of God are these few words, that it would be impossible to terminate the greatest of all mysteries in a more becoming manner.

"What," says St. Augustine, "can we think, "say, or write, better than those words,—Thanks "be to God? We cannot say anything shorter, "more agreeable, more noble, more useful, more "beneficial."

Yes, thanks be to God! for heaven and earth are now reconciled; the august Victim, expected during four thousand years, has this moment been immolated. It has been received by God as a Sacrifice and by men as a Sacrament. Thanks be to God the Father, who has given us His Son. Thanks to God the Son, who has taken upon Him our nature. Thanks to God the Holy Ghost, who has sanctified us in Jesus Christ. Thanks to the august Trinity, for all its gifts and mercies, of which this Catholic Sacrifice is the abridgment.

We should leave the house of God as our predecessors in the faith used to do; an impression of holiness should, during the whole day, reign in our thoughts, words, desires, and actions. Let us remember that heaven, earth, and hell have their eyes fixed upon us; heaven, to rejoice at our having assisted at the great Sacrifice; earth, to be edified at our demeanour; and hell, to deprive us of the fruits of the Sacrifice. Let us not rejoice hell; let us not grieve heaven; let us not cause the Christian name to be blasphemed among men. Let us spend the day as if we had that morning witnessed the Sacrifice of Calvary. Let us leave the house of God as if we were descending from that Mount. Let us not, like the Jews, become more blind and more hardened after this spectacle. Let us rather, like the centurion, publish and proclaim the glory of the Son of God. Let us, like the multitude, after having witnessed what has taken place, return, striking our breasts.

SUMMARY OR RESUMÉ

OF THE ABOVE TREATISE.

The Mass is an adorable, awful Sacrifice, replete with the Divinity.

I. Christ came down from heaven and took upon Him our nature, to make us partakers of His Divinity, and carry us up to heaven.

II. He offered Himself up a Sacrifice on the Cross, to deliver us from sin and hell; and to purchase for us mercy, grace, and salvation.

III. In order to communicate to all future generations of mankind the merits and fruits of the Sacrifice of the Cross, He instituted the Sacrifice of the Mass, which is a continuation of the Sacrifice of the Cross, nay, the same Sacrifice and a real representation and commemoration thereof.

IV. The two great objects of the Mass, the two great ends for which it was instituted, are, —1. To communicate to all future generations of mankind to the end of time, the benefits, fruits, and merits of the Sacrifice of the Cross;

and 2. To enable them to render to God, in a manner worthy of Him, the four great duties that we owe to Him, of adoration, thanksgiving, atonement, and impetration.

V. Jesus Christ is, in the Mass, the principal High Priest and invisible worker, to whose command everything is obedient, while the visible priest is but His minister, acting in His Name and Person, and by His authority.

VI. During the Mass, we should always bear in mind that it is a God who is the chief Priest of this Sacrifice, a God who is the Victim, and a God to whom it is offered up.

VII. From the consecration to the end of the communion, we should endeavour to entertain a lively faith of the Divine Presence on our altars, together with a religious dread, fear, and awe thereof, and a deep sense of our own unworthiness.

VIII. Our outward bearing, especially during the above part of the service, should be such as to convince all present, of our conviction and sense of the Divine Presence on our altars.

IX. The Eucharist, as a sacrament, is the remedy of all our evils, the most powerful medicine for all our diseases, the sovereign antidote against the poison of the infernal serpent, the comfort of our banishment, the support of our pilgrimage, the price of our ransom, the earnest of our eternal salvation.

THE END.

www.ingramcontent.com/pod-product-compliance
Lightning Source LLC
Chambersburg PA
CBHW030325240426
43673CB00040B/1282